freeform Wire Art jewelry

Techniques for designing with wire, beads and gems

Gayle Bird

Fons&Porter

Cincinnati, OH

contents

Introduction

I absolutely love working with wire. If it's not nailed down, it's likely I'll eventually try wrapping it in wire! This book is the result of fifteen years of experiments, failures, and re-tries. I've done all the trying and failing so you don't have to!

When I was approached to write this book, I was elated. I truly believe that anyone can learn to make their own jewelry; more than that, I believe that everyone can create their own style. Most new artists learn the same techniques from the same batch of online tutorials. As a result, much of what beginners make ends up looking the same as everyone else. But it doesn't have to be that way! With a bit of freedom and plenty of solid techniques, you can learn to create your own style and begin making jewelry that is instantly recognizable as yours alone.

This book is set up more like a textbook or class than a random assortment of projects. The beginning of the book focuses on unconventional tools, design techniques, color theory, improvisation and a series of foundational techniques that are referred to in the projects and used as the basis of many an improvisation. Each project is interconnected, and the projects later in the book assume you have completed the earlier projects.

I am convinced that you'll find the text easy to follow, the projects uncomplicated, and that if you complete the whole book, you'll effortlessly begin working towards your own remarkable design style. See for yourself!

The Basics

It can be tempting to dive right into the projects in a book like this, but it's important that you take the time to review the basics first. I strongly believe that you need to understand your materials and your tools before you pick them up; and that you need to understand color and design before you can create anything significant. I've been teaching color and design for nearly fifteen years and trust me, this is only a small segment of the subject.

Copper-core wire plated with silver

Wire

CHOOSING THE RIGHT WIRE

Wire has been sparking my imagination for more than a decade. My first wire project popped fully formed into my brain, and it was so spontaneous that I literally used garbage bag ties stripped of their paper. The results were less than perfect but sometimes creativity just won't wait!

After that I tried whatever I could get my hands on: beading wire (too soft), brass wire from the hardware store (too hard), even soldering wire (not structurally sound), and eventually some silver-plated wire. I wasn't fully satisfied with any of them, and I've since come up with a few requirements:

1. Materials shouldn't be so expensive that they stifle creativity.

2. The wire should support both broad strokes and tiny details.

3. Finished pieces should be easy to clean.

I've now found a wire that's up to my standards: copper-core wire plated with pure silver or perma- nently enameled with antiqued colors, and then coated with poly-nylon. It's inexpensive, so I don't have to worry about wasting it while I'm designing; it's workable in any way I'd like (and can be work-hardened easily), perfect for intricate details as well as large motifs; and it never tarnishes, so I don't have to worry about cleaning the wire. An added bonus is that the wire is soft: it doesn't hurt my hands when I work it. It's like a miracle wire!

Wire comes in many gauges, which can be confus- ing. The basic thing to remember is that the bigger the number, the smaller the wire. We'll mostly be using wire in the 18–22ga range. There are many brands you can try, such as Parawire, Artistic Wire and Zebra Wire.

A quick online search for "colored wire" or a trip to your local craft store should get you started. The coated wire comes on spools of about 25' (7.6m). Feel free to use any kind of wire you like, but be aware that if you're using fine metals, measuring accurately and using scraps becomes important, not something covered in this book.

Tools

I've listed the essential tools here, but you already own the most important tool of all: your hands. Many of the techniques in this book depend extensively on using your hands. Becoming less dependent on the use of tools is a big part of what will give your work that organic, freeform look.

As for the quality of your tools, any no-name brand from the hardware or big box store will do for now, but once you become seriously interested in producing more than one or two pieces a week, and as soon as you can afford to do so, upgrade. Just as with computers and cars, buy the very best you can afford. With proper care, your tools will last a long time.

ESSENTIAL TOOLS

Whenever I take my wire on the road with me, I bring along four sets of pliers. I can fudge the rest.

Side Cutters. These are the first pliers you'll touch as you need them to cut the wire off the spool. Side cutters have a flat side and a deep "v" side—always cut with the flat side up against your work so the ends are as flat as possible. If you invest in any high-end tools, start with your cutters; they'll make your ends neater and will be kinder on your hands.

Bent Chain-Nose Pliers. You'll use these flat, tapered pliers with a hook at the end for gripping and bending wire. In my opinion, bent chain-nose pliers are better than regular chain-nose pliers because their angle allows you to hold your wrists in a more comfortable position. The more delicate the tips, the better. Never use the serrated-jaw pliers you can buy at the hardware store.

Round-Nose Pliers. Tapered, round-barreled pliers will help with making spirals. Look for pliers with a very fine tip: they make the best spirals. You can also use round-nose pliers to make loops and curls, but you'll primarily use your hands for that in this book.

Bail-Making Pliers. Thick, straight-barreled, round pliers which will help you create bails for hanging

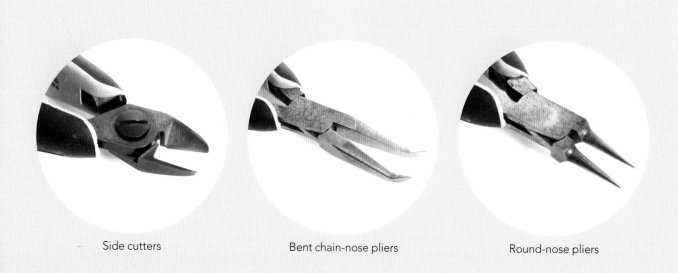

Side cutters · Bent chain-nose pliers · Round-nose pliers

your work from a chain. These come in many sizes, from tiny to huge. I tend to use the medium-sized ones. You can use round-nose pliers to make bails as well, but using bail-making pliers is much easier.

HELPFUL TOOLS

These tools are helpful, but not required to complete all projects.

Flat-Nose Pliers. Wide, flat pliers with square ends, these will help flatten wire across broad surfaces and work well in conjunction with the bent-nose pliers. You might find nylon-jaw flat-nose pliers useful, as well.

Hammer and Anvil. A simple hammering surface and a flat hammer can help you work-harden your wire. Many craft stores carry simple jewelry hammers and anvil blocks. You can also work-harden your pieces by compressing wire with nylon-jaw flat-nose pliers.

There are many other types of pliers, such as split-ring pliers, crimping pliers, mandrel pliers, and other specialty pliers. As you get comfortable using the basics, explore the other options that are out there and find what works best for you.

CARING FOR YOUR TOOLS

Your tools are an investment and you need to take care of them. Keep metal tools oiled and clean. Store them in a dry place so they won't rust, and don't use them past their tolerance or intended use.

You must also care for your hands; take frequent breaks and stretch them out between sessions. Avoid doing the exact same motion repeatedly for extended periods of time.

BASIC TOOL USAGE

Hold pliers lightly, with one handle along the length of your thumb and the other lightly controlled with your fingers. Don't grip too hard; you will damage both the wire and your hands if you exert too much pressure. Always use a light touch. You may find you tuck your pinky and/or ring finger inside the handles at times to get better control.

When using pliers to make loops, it's important that you keep full contact between the wire and the pliers to avoid malformed loops.

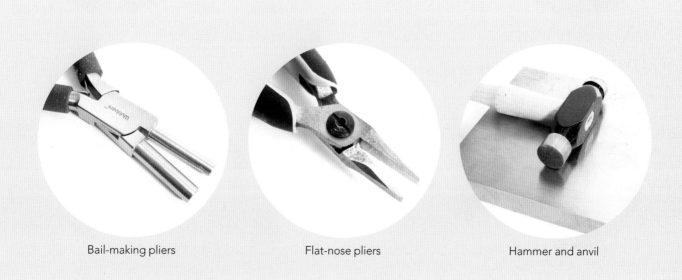

Bail-making pliers   Flat-nose pliers   Hammer and anvil

Color Theory

One of my absolute favorite parts of making jewelry is playing with the color combinations. A solid understanding of color theory will help you make informed decisions when creating earrings and multi-stone pendants or necklaces, and you'll gain an understanding of how to match the color of your wire to the color of your elements.

The basis of all color theory is the color wheel. You can choose a traditional color wheel or an alternate one; both have twelve colors.

The **traditional color wheel** is based on three colors which are used to build all the other colors. The three **primary** colors are red, yellow and blue. You can't create these colors by mixing other colors together; they're what make every other color possible. Mixing any two primary colors creates a **secondary** color: green (blue and yellow), purple (red and blue) and orange (red and yellow). Mix a secondary with a primary color and you'll get the **tertiary** colors: yellow-green, blue-green, blue-purple, red-purple, red-orange and yellow-orange.

The **alternate color wheel** uses a base of yellow, magenta and cyan (the primary colors). You can work from either wheel; I like bright magentas and purples, so my examples will often use the alternate wheel. Just as with the traditional wheel, the alternate wheel has primary, secondary and tertiary colors.

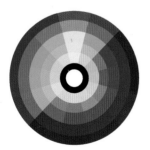

Traditional Color Wheel

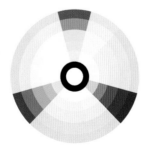

Primary

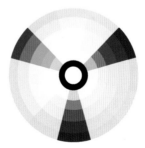

Secondary

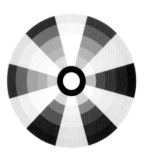

Tertiary

Alternate Color Wheel

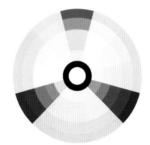

Alternate Primary

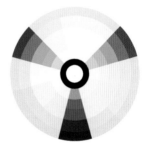

Alternate Secondary

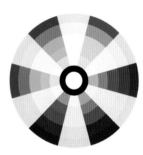

Alternate Tertiary

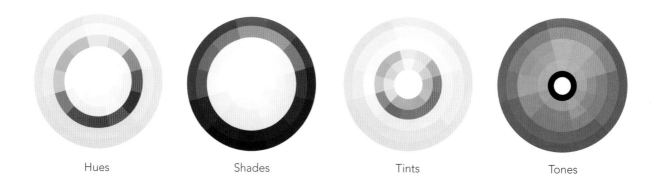

| Hues | Shades | Tints | Tones |

COLOR VALUE

The pure version of a color is called the **hue**; it's untainted by black or white. Start with the hue when picking colors.

If you darken a hue by adding black, it's called a **shade**. If you lighten a hue by adding white, it's called a **tint**. A **tone** is a hue with both black and white (gray) added, tending towards neutrality, or a hue with some strength of its complementary color added.

COLOR INTENSITY

Also known as saturation, intensity describes the strength of the color. A soft pink is low intensity while neon pink is highly saturated and very intense. When choosing colors, think about how strong and intense that color is and whether or not that fits with the theme of your design. Is your theme soft and romantic? Try lower intensity colors.

NEUTRALS

Black, white, gray, brown and extremely toned down colors (with gray added) are all neutral colors. The purpose of a neutral color is to allow your focal colors to be framed and intensified. Wire will often serve as a neutral in your design.

If you use black with pure warm colors, it can help the colors look even more vibrant and alive. Using white with warm colors can wash out the warmth, but using white with cooler colors can be perfect. Experiment with various neutrals to find what works for you.

Saturation of Pinks

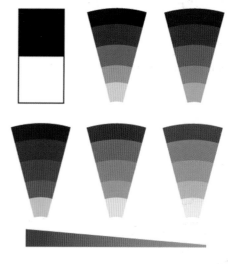

Neutrals

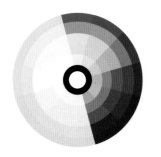

Warm Colors   Cool Colors

COLOR TEMPERATURE

Warm colors have a yellow undertone: red, orange, yellow, green-yellow, etc. These colors lend a sense of warmth, comfort, and energy to the color selection, and tend to stand out and come forward in a design.

Cool colors have a blue undertone: blue, violet, aqua, green, etc. These colors stabilize and cool the color scheme, and tend to recede in a design.

COLOR CONTRAST

Contrast is the difference between two colors and can be created by contrasting hue, value and saturation, or any combination of these. Contrast is one of the most important things to keep in mind when working on the color in your design, as it's what will keep the design from being flat.

COLOR SCHEMES

Now let's talk about how to pick colors for a design. Find color inspiration in nature, current trends, a specific outfit, artwork or a photo, or even a specific focal piece. For the beginner, color harmony schemes can be an excellent way to start. Color harmony is a set of rules to help you create harmonious color combinations.

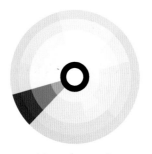

Monochromatic

Monochromatic

A monochromatic scheme is the easiest and simplest of the color harmonies. It uses hues (variations in shade and tint) of a single color. This creates a simple, clean, classy design that creates natural color contrast and interest. When you use a single hue in a design, create contrast in the design by using a mixture of dark and light shades, different finishes on similar beads, or different shapes and sizes.

Analogous

This scheme uses three to five colors adjacent to each other on the color wheel. These work because they have common primary colors. The colors are neighbours, which makes the whole scheme quiet and pleasant. Choose a predominant color to establish a base, and use the others as accents to maintain the soothing appearance. Nature is full of analogous themes such as blue-green oceans or red-brown timbers.

Complementary

This scheme consists of two colors, opposite each other on the color wheel, and is an extremely difficult scheme to pull off properly. Red and green for Christmas is the most common of these schemes. Using complementary colors can make each color appear brighter and more vibrant, but be sure you don't use equal amounts; the color contrast on complementary hues is usually too strong.

Other types of complementary colors can be simpler to work with than straight complementary combinations:

Near complementary: Instead of picking the color exactly opposite your starting color, choose a color next to the opposite. It can be more interesting and easier on the eyes.

Split complementary: Choose a color, and then pick both colors next to its opposite.

Analogous complentary: Choose two colors side by side, and then include a hue directly opposite.

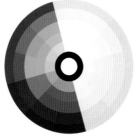

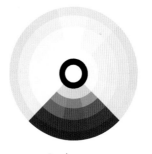

Analogous

Complementary

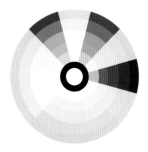

Modified Triadic

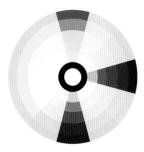

Complementary Triadic

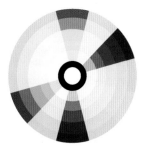

Rectangle Tetradic

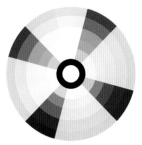

Square Tetradic

Triadic

This color harmony uses three colors evenly spaced around the 12-color wheel. Primary colors are triadic; so are secondary colors. The visual contrast is strong but balanced: it is subtler and richer than the complementary scheme, and much more harmonious.

Modified triadic: Choose three colors one space apart instead of two spaces.

Complementary triadic: Combine any two complements with one of the two available colors halfway between them on the wheel.

Tetradic

My favorite way to pick colors, this scheme is exremtely rich and, due to its very contrasting nature, forces you to choose a dominant color to keep the balance. Tetradic schemes are four colors from the wheel chosen in two ways:

Rectangle Tetradic: Choose four colors arranged into two complementary pairs, forming a rectangle.

Square Tetradic: Instead of two complementary sets one space apart, pick four colors spaced evenly around the wheel in a square.

COMBINING COLORS

If you use all your chosen colors at full intensity, the colors will compete with each other, creating an unharmonious and uninteresting design. When everything is the same strength, nothing is strong. Instead, choose variations on pure-hue color schemes to create lively, interesting schemes. Use tints or shades, or contrast the saturation and lightness to increase your options. This not only reduces the contrast, which is easier on the eyes, but also creates a lovely balance that is difficult to create with solid colors.

Use colors in decreasing proportions: choose a single color to be the dominant color in a design, use less of a second color, and only a small amount of the third and fourth.

You can also use spacing to counteract the heavy contrast between two colors. Red and blue together at full intensity can cause a visual dissonance that is unpleasant to the eye, so it's usually best avoided. Lots of companies do use red and blue in their logos, but they're almost always separated by white.

CONCLUSION

Color is often the first thing visible in your designs; pay it special attention. Learn the rules of color, use them deliberately. Your work will be better for it.

Design Principles

In addition to color, there are a few things to keep in mind when planning the layout of a piece of jewelry. It may seem backwards to plan color before a design, but it's often what drives your inspiration. Now that you understand color theory, let's look at the rules that can help you create a balanced, intriguing design.

GESTALT

This word means "the whole," and it refers to how the piece flows as a unit. The idea behind gestalt is to make sure that you have just the right amount of unity and variety. If your design is too unified, it can be boring; too varied, and it can be chaotic. There are several parts to this concept; let's review them quickly:

Closure

Continuance

Similarity

Proximity

Closure

Your brain is an amazing tool. If something is missing visually, your brain fills in what's missing, allowing you to see the whole picture. This is called closure. Applied to jewelry design, a partial curve in a design can be construed as a full circle by the viewer. Leaving a gap in a piece will add interest without interrupting the design.

Continuance

The eye can be drawn along the length of a design, compelled to look in the direction you choose based on the lines and groupings you build. You can use this to point the eye towards your focal point(s).

Similarity

When objects look similar, they are grouped visually even if they're not necessarily close together. By repeating elements throughout your design, you create cohesion. This can mean using the same beads, same colors, same wire color or same textures across the design. In addition, if you have many similar elements, you can use them to place focus on another, dissimilar element.

Proximity

When things are close together, they seem to belong together. If you scatter beads evenly throughout a design, for instance, they can seem disconnected; groupings are much more effective.

tips & hints

I often figure out gestalt by squinting my eyes and seeing how the design looks slightly out of focus. Other tricks are to look at the piece in a mirror or to look at it from far away. Using any of these tricks, you can identify problems with balance, focus, contrast and more.

CONTRAST

To achieve gestalt, there are many concepts and principles you can apply, but most of them can be talked about in terms of contrast. We've already talked about color contrast, but you'll want to keep an eye on contrast of size (balance), materials, texture and weight. Use differences in these qualities to deliberately move the eye and draw focus where you want it.

Proportion

Proportion is the visual division of elements; how much of one versus how much of another. A simpler term for proportion is balance. Balance is both visual and physical. Dangly earrings, for instance, need to physically balance when they hang. A neckpiece needs to balance on the neck and not fall off or overweight in one direction. But the way a piece looks should also be balanced. There are a few things to keep in mind when looking for balance:

Symmetrical vs Asymmetrical: Unless I'm working on a formal piece, I rarely make symmetrical designs. Though symmetry is soothing and solid, it's also staid. Who wants staid jewelry? Visually, it can be boring. When I balance my pieces, I make sure they're asymmetrically balanced, which means that the visual weight on both sides of the center line is equal, although not identical. For instance, I might make a giant triple curl bottom right, and three tiny curls opposite, top left, to balance it out.

In this book you'll find asymmetrical designs almost exclusively. You should be able to identify and create both symmetrical and asymmetrical designs, and more often, a combination of the two. For instance, a neckpiece should be symmetrical in structure, but its decoration can be asymmetrical.

Rule of Thirds: Three is sort of a magic number. Even numbers don't work well in jewelry design; they're too solid. Almost all artists will work in threes by creating clusters of three beads, divisions of three pieces, or by putting the focus of a piece a third of the way down or a third of the way over.

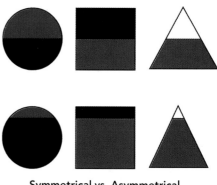

Symmetrical vs. Asymmetrical
Top: Boring, symmetrical balance
Bottom: Asymmetrical, but unbalanced

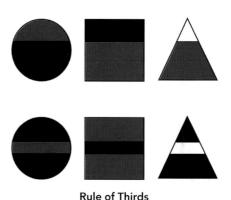

Rule of Thirds
Top: One-third to two-thirds is a pleasing balance
Bottom: Balance can be distributed

Weight

If you're using a really heavy focal piece, you will probably need heavy wire to support it both physically and visually. However, if you also add a fine wire to the mix, by coiling it around a piece of the heavy wire or working it alongside, you'll add energy to the piece.

If you have a piece that feels bland, try adding something with different weight. Contrast a grouping of tiny clusters against a single, chunky element.

Shape

Contrast round with sharp, square with curved, flat with volume. Balance the proportion of the shapes with one another.

Texture

Use different materials to create interest in your piece; contrast smooth with rough, ragged with curved. The proportion of textures you use should be balanced and in proportion with one another.

Steps to Creating a Jewelry Design

Now that you understand the concepts behind a great design, it's time to pull it all together. I usually look through my bead stash for a focal piece, choose a style or theme for the piece, pick other materials to go with the focal piece (usually beads of a certain color scheme) and then play with the materials to find a layout I like. From there I move into working with wire and deciding how the elements will go together. Of course you can work any way you please but this is what I recommend:

1. Select a focal piece

2. Choose a color scheme

3. Pick supporting materials

4. Lay out your design

5. Build the piece

CHOOSE A FOCAL PIECE

Usually you'll have a focal piece you want to work with: a piece of beach glass, a gorgeous lampworked bead, or something you've created out of clay. It should be something that inspires you; something intriguing, something that speaks to you for some reason. It doesn't need to be flawless; it just needs to grab your attention, because that is its purpose in the piece.

Examine the Focal

Decide if you want a lot going on with color and texture throughout the piece, or if the focal piece is going to stand alone with the wire as its only support. If you decide to use accent colors, examine the focal piece and analyze its colors. Is it a single hue, variations on a hue, monochromatic, analogous, triadic or tetradic? Write down the colors if necessary.

Now, inspect the proportions of these colors. What is the balance? Maybe it's 90 percent one color with tiny flecks of something you can pick up in your accent beads, or maybe the central color is hard to pick out because the colors are evenly proportioned. Is there one main color, one secondary color, and one smaller accent color, or is it more like a crazy quilt with all the colors equally represented? Look closely; sometimes the smallest vein of matrix in a stone can turn into a stunning focus on the piece simply by picking up the same color in your supporting materials.

Once you have a working concept of how the focal colors are represented, you can move on to choosing the supporting colors.

CHOOSE A COLOR SCHEME

Decide on your theme: Is the piece meant to be bold, adventurous, playful, romantic, earthy, subtle, airy, dense? Based on your gut feeling about the piece, pick a color scheme, realizing that those with colors closer to each other on the wheel (with fewer contrasts) are softer and simpler, while the ones from all over the wheel are more exciting and complex.

Find the main color you've identified from your focal piece on the color wheel. If you can't find the exact color, look for the closest approximation. Use the color scheme you've chosen to pick accent colors by finding the related colors on the wheel.

CHOOSE A WIRE COLOR

Artistic wire comes in many colors. I use mainly silver and traditional antiqued metal colors rather than the whole rainbow of colors available. In my work, I like the wire to support the beads and components, not steal the show.

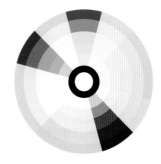

Traditional Complementary
Color Scheme

Traditional Split Complementary
Color Scheme

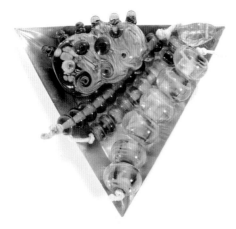

Based on color theory, I often pair silver with cool colors and antiqued metal with warmer colors. But you'd be surprised what can happen when you put brown wire on a blue stone! Experiment and see what you like.

LAY OUT THE DESIGN

Now comes the fun part! Open up your bead and component stash and with the focal piece in hand, start looking for the colors you've chosen. Be sure to compare the beads with the actual focal color; cyan is not cobalt and if you aren't careful, you can pick clashing colors. Grab a handful of anything that might work.

Dump the beads onto your working surface and group the colors. Do you like the proportions of the colors? Move the groups around, break them up, and most especially, play with the beads by rearranging them around your focal piece until you arrive at a layout that is balanced and harmonious.

BUILD

Now that you have an actual plan, it's time to pick up your tools and get to work. You need to think about both form and function—which simply means you can't just think about how the piece looks, but how it works as well. Does it need a clasp, or a bail, or a pin back? How will you integrate these functional pieces? Plan it out. Visualize it in your head, or sketch out the functional pieces on paper. A plan will save you from tearing a piece apart and starting again because it isn't stable or the clasp doesn't work!

The following techniques and projects are designed to ensure that you're able to adapt them to nearly any situation. So play! Experiment. Create your own style.

Techniques

This section is the heart of the book; the projects that come later are the soul. You need both to create compelling pieces! Here you'll learn the techniques any wire worker will recognize and use daily, and you'll be let in on the secrets to my signature "swirls." You'll also get to practice improvisation, so you can transform the projects in this book into one-of-a-kind pieces. Finally, I'll show you how to bring everything together with a quick project that combines the skills you've learned thus far.

Before you try the organic decorations and projects, it's important you're comfortable working with wire. With that in mind, practice the techniques below until you're able to do them easily. Experienced wire workers can skip ahead to the Organic Wire Techniques. Everyone else, grab some practice wire and let's get started!

CUT

It's very important that you use the flat side of your side cutters to create a very flat, flush cut. If you cut with the V-shaped profile facing down, you will end up with a V-shaped end instead of a flat end on your wire. Make a few practice cuts to your wire.

STRAIGHTEN

Most wire comes on spools. When you remove wire from a spool, don't pull it up off the top of a stationary spool like you might with yarn; kinks can form. Instead, unroll it from the spool by pulling sideways and letting the spool spin, like you would with a paper towel roll.

Once it's off the spool, the wire will likely have a slight curve. Run your fingers very lightly along the length of the wire to straighten it out. If you do this several times, or if you use nylon-jaw pliers to straighten the wire, you'll get a straighter wire but it will also be harder. This can be useful if you need very straight, stiff wires, but most of the projects in this book require soft wire, so straightening it once with your fingers will suffice.

BEND

To create a sharp, 90-degree bend in your wire, place your flat-nose or bent chain-nose pliers with the edge facing you at the point where you want the bend. Push your thumb against the wire at this edge. With a sharp motion, bend the pliers away from you while pushing gently with your thumb to make a precise edge. If the wire curves a bit on either side of the bend, use your flat-nose pliers to straighten the wire as close to the bend as possible, on both sides.

Use the flat side of the cutters.

Use your fingers to straighten the wire.

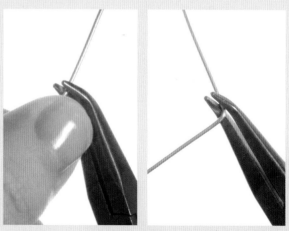

Create a bend with flat-nose or chain-nose pliers.

EYE LOOP

The eye loop is a simple, useful technique. The loop itself is useful as a connector, but the technique involves round-nose or (as pictured) bail-making pliers, for which the same basic technique applies when creating bails and other connectors.

1 Hold the bail-making pliers with the mandrel side you plan to use on top (in this case, the larger), and grasp the very end of your wire between the 2 jaws of the pliers. The tip of the wire should just be visible where the 2 jaws meet.

2 Rotate the pliers over the wire, away from you, until the wire touches the bottom jaw (which is now on top).

3 Loosen your grip on the pliers and reposition the smaller jaw further back on the wire end. Grasp it gently again and continue the looping motion until the wire end is touching the tail end of the wire. The place where the loop touches is called the neck.

4 Loosen your grip again and twist the pliers all the way back so the smaller jaw is touching the neck.

5 Grasp the wire again and bend the pliers backwards, away from the neck, until the loop is sitting centered on the neck.

6 Remove the loop from the pliers. You're done!

tips & hints

It's important that the loop sits nicely on the neck. Malformed loops are unstable and unattractive, as shown.

It's also important to balance the weight of the wire with the size of the pliers you're using. In the photo to the right, the large loop on the left is an 18ga wire made on the larger side of the medium bail-making pliers. It is well balanced and relatively strong. The middle loop is made using the same size pliers but with a much smaller 22ga wire. This loop is unstable and will

collapse easily. The final loop is the same 22ga wire on the smaller jaw of the bailmaking pliers; a well-balanced and very strong eye loop.

WRAPPED EYE LOOP

For a truly strong loop connector, make a wrapped eye loop. The regular eye loop has a flaw: it can be opened. The wrapped eye loop is permanently closed and extremely stable.

1 Grasp the wire about 1"–1½" (2.5cm–3.8cm) down from the end of the wire and begin a loop the same as with the eye loop.

2 This time, when you adjust your grip, allow the tail wire to cross over itself and create a 90-degree angle with the neck.

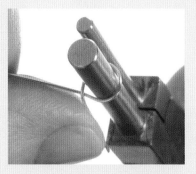

3 Use your thumb to push the tail wire around the neck.

4 Wrap once, keeping the wire loop touching the pliers as closely as possible.

5 Grab a second set of pliers (flat-nose or, as I prefer, bent chain-nose) and continue the wrap. Pull the wire from the end; you'll have good control over the placement of the wire. If the wrap doesn't seem tight enough, gently coax it into place using your bent chain-nose or flat-nose pliers with a light grip perpendicular to the neck and a rotational motion in the direction of the wrap.

6 Wrap 3 or 5 times and finish the wrap by cutting the tail flush and close to the neck.

7 Use that same rotational motion to gently tamp down the wire end against the neck with the flat-nose pliers. You'll use this tucking/tamping technique many times.

8 Remove the loop from the pliers.

BINDING WRAP

Binding wraps are an excellent way to connect two pieces together. Here we'll practice with two scraps of copper wire. Usually you'll want your binding wire to be somewhat thinner (higher gauge) than the wire you're binding together.

1 Find or cut some 18–20ga scrap wire. Create bends in each element wire to simulate the curves found in the projects.

2 Cut a longer piece of 22–24ga wire, about 5" (12.7cm) long (you'll have extra!). Place the thin wire against the 2 pieces you're wrapping together, with a 1"–2" (2.5cm–5.1cm) tail sticking out.

3 Bend the tail behind the element wires and hold it tight along with the element wires in your nondominant hand. It's important you don't let this wire slip.

4 Wrap the thin wire around the element wires twice.

5 Use your bent chain-nose pliers to gently tighten the wrap and adjust the wrapped wires so they lie flat and close together.

6 Continue wrapping the binding wire. You will find it easiest to wrap if you make a little "handle" bend in the tail.

7 When the wrap is the length you want (at least 3 wraps for stability) use your bent chain-nose or flat-nose pliers to push the wraps together if necessary.

8 If available, wrap the end of your wire 3 times around a single element wire to finish it off. This will make the wrap more secure. Don't cut it yet.

9 Flip the piece around. Note that the initial wrap is loose and imprecise; use your pliers to tighten it up against the element wires and the wrap wire.

10 Cut the tail wire close to the wrap at the back of the piece (the same side, in this case).

11 Gently tamp down the ends by rotating lightly around the wrap in its same direction. Give a final clamp-down over all the wraps to harden them.

12 Cut and tamp down the first wire after it's been tightened. The binding wrap is complete!

OPEN SPIRAL

This is a basic embellishment that can be used in many different ways.
The round-nose pliers with smaller tips will work best for a spiral.

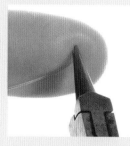   

1 Use the very tip of your smallest round-nose pliers and grasp the very tip of the end of your wire. Use your nondominant hand to stabilize the wire.

2 With a sharp flick of your wrist, create a tiny P at the end of the wire. For best results, keep full contact between the wire and the pliers.

3 Dividing the motion between your 2 wrists, rotate the pliers tightly until the pliers get in the way, while curling the wire up and over in the opposite direction.

4 Continue turning the wire with the pliers. You may need to release your grip and re-grip with the pliers.

TWIST

Twisting wires together is a quick way to attach them, although it's
not appropriate for every application. It's important that you twist
them equally and don't end up with one wrapped around the other.
The placement of your hands is the key to this technique.

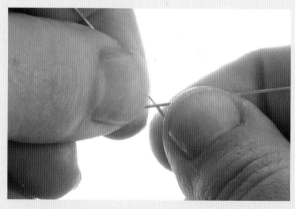

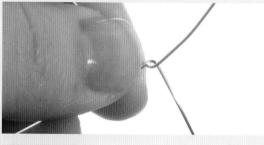

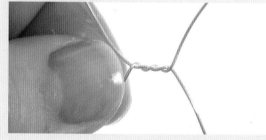

1 Where the 2 wires cross, grasp each side of the X they make with the thumb and forefinger of each hand. Your thumbs should be essentially pointing straight at each other, centered directly in the middle of the X, and your forefingers should also be grasping the X in the center. Your thumbs should be touching and your forefingers touching each other as well (even closer than in this photo, in which I pulled back so you could see the X).

2 Twist your wrists in opposite directions, pushing your thumbs gently towards each other to keep the twist straight and true. The wires should be equally twisted around each other on a diagonal, not 1 straight and the other wrapped around. Repeat the twist at least 3 times for stability.

Organic Wire Techniques

The look we're going for with these wire projects is an organic, hand-made elegance: think of these decorations as drawing with wire. The ability to do this comes from instinct, but the instinct is built from practice and a series of basic "moves" that are chained together to build complex, unique designs. We'll work on the basic structures first and then show you how to improvise!

THE CURL

Here's the first truly organic shape you'll make: the curl. It forms the basis of all the other curlicues, so practice! Take careful note of the finger positions at each step.

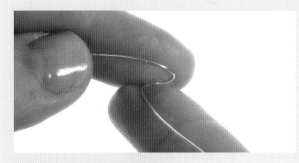

1 Lightly grasp a piece of wire near the middle in your nondominant hand, palm up. Most of the pressure will be between your thumb and forefinger. With your dominant hand palm down, grasp the other half of the wire even more loosely; don't even really grab it at all with this hand, just guide it with your fingers. Press the tip of your forefingers together with the wire between them.

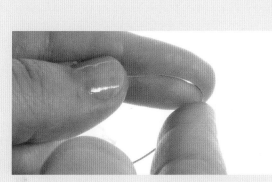

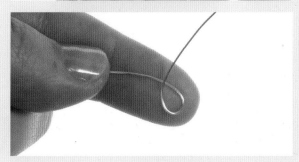

2 The tip of your dominant finger is where the curl will be formed. Press the wire between both forefingers, sliding your dominant finger along the wire and outward, away from your body. Guiding the wire with both hands, rotate your dominant finger outward in the same direction. This will start the curl.

3 Keep rotating your hands, with full contact between both forefingers, until your nondominant palm is facing down and your dominant palm is facing up. Your nondominant hand pushes the wire curl up and over while your dominant hand guides it. The curl should now be formed between your fingers.

THE DOUBLE CURL

The double curl is the second fundamental skill you need to master in order to move into a true improvisational style of your own. It looks complicated, but as the name suggests, it's simply two curls on top of each other!

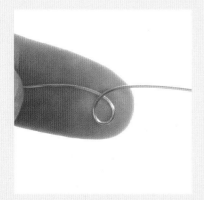

1 Create a single curl as instructed in the previous lesson.

2 Repeat the curl-making process over top of the first curl using a larger rotation. A double curl is created.

THE ALTERNATE CURL

The first curl you learned to make is pointing down. To quickly create chains of alternating curls, let's learn to make one pointing up.

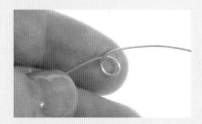

1 Create a single curl in the middle of a piece of wire.

2 Keep hold of the curl in the starting position, resting it against the forefinger of your nondominant hand. Use your dominant thumb to gently start the alternate curl by pushing it down slightly, guiding the wire with your fingers.

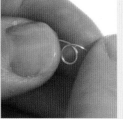
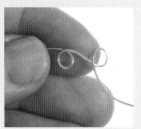

3 Put your nondominant forefinger into the indentation you've just created; with your dominant forefinger, draw upward with the wire, starting a new curl.

4 Push the curl into your nondominant forefinger, rotating your hands the opposite way of the original curl so your nondominant hand ends up on top, pushing the curl backwards.

CHAINING CURLS

The impact of a curl is increased when you chain them together, creating multiple curls on the same piece of wire. You can create a chain of alternate curls or keep all the curls facing the same direction.

Remember the basic rules of design; in this case, you want to balance your curls and work in groups of three, five or seven.

Alternate curl chain

Repeated curl chain

IMPROVISE

Now comes the fun part: improvisation! See if you can duplicate the designs shown below, and then using several pieces of practice wire, keep trying different configurations. Note the balance and asymmetry. See how the various designs can be placed across different sizes and shapes of stones and elements. Watch your balance and proportion.

Improvised Designs

Easy Curls Necklace

In this simple project, choose one of your practice wires and try out a few basic techniques while also creating an instantly wearable necklace.

TOOLS + MATERIALS

- decorated heavy practice wire
- 6" (15cm) of heavy gauge wire
- chain
- 2 jump rings
- large-barreled round-nose pliers
- bail-making pliers
- bent chain-nose pliers
- flat-nose pliers
- side cutters

1 Choose a heavy piece of wire decorated with curls (or create a new one). Using your large-barreled round-nose pliers (or bail-making pliers), grasp the very end of the wire to start an eye loop at 1 end.

2 Using your wrist, turn the pliers, wrapping the wire around the barrel tightly, until the end of the wire touches the neck of the loop.

3 Repeat on the other side of the decorative wire so you have an eye loop on either end. Curve the piece slightly so it creates a gentle U shape.

tips & hints

The decorations in this practice necklace aren't as stable as other methods; you can strengthen the wire by gently tapping it with a rubber or nylon mallet against a nonmetal surface such as a wood or rubber block, or by gently putting pressure on the loops and open wires with flat-nose nylon-jaw pliers.

4 Open both of the loops sideways.

5 Decide your necklace length; this style works well resting on the collarbone. Subtract the length of your decorative wire and another inch (2.5cm) for the clasp from your desired length. Cut a piece of chain to that length, then cut it exactly in half. Thread the end of each piece of chain onto an open loop.

6 Close up the loops using bent chain-nose pliers.

7 To make the clasp, cut a length of wire about 6"–8" (15.2cm–20.3cm) long. With heavy wire such as this 18-ga, it's important to have the flattest cut possible.

8 Use the tip of your round-nose pliers to create a small loop at the end of the wire.

9 Place the small loop into your bail-making pliers, and create another loop around the large barrel in the opposite direction from the small loop.

10 About ½" (1.3cm) from the bottom of the small loop, create a 90-degree bend in the tail of the wire.

11 Create a small loop in the opposite direction of the bend.

12 Turn the loop into a wrapped loop: wrap the tail wire around the neck of the small loop (leaving the wire on the round-nose pliers will make this easier), and cut and tuck in the end of the wire on the inside of the clasp.

13 Open a heavy jump ring using 2 pairs of pliers (flat-nose and bent chain-nose shown here), twisting each wrist in opposite directions so the jump ring opens sideways (don't bend the circle out of shape).

14 Slip 1 of the chain ends attached to your decorated wire and the wrapped loop end of the clasp onto the jump ring, then close the ring using the opposite motion with your 2 sets of pliers.

15 Attach a similar jump ring to the other end of the wire to act as the other end of the clasp. You've now built a hook-and-eye clasp, and you have an interesting, simple necklace to wear!

The Projects

This section of the book is where you'll put together everything you've learned so far about wire, improvisation, color and design, and begin making truly original work. We start with the easiest techniques for earrings and rings, move into making pendants and handling doubled wire, and work our way up to a magnificent, custom statement necklace.

The progression of techniques is deliberate and should be followed in order. If you can't help yourself and you jump ahead, you may find that the project you're working on relies on a technique taught earlier! So take the time to work through the earrings, then rings, then pendants, and finally the necklaces. You'll end up with a beautiful repertoire of jewelry and a stable of techniques that you can use in your own designs!

Easy Teardrop Earrings

The most basic projects can have the most stunning results. Here, a matched pair of beads and a wrapped loop become enchantingly simple teardrop earrings. The trick is to treat the two wires as a single wire; you'll get identical shapes without too much fuss, and avoid marring the wire.

TOOLS + MATERIALS
- 22ga wire, about 12"–14" (30.5cm–35.6cm)
- Two 10mm beads
- 2 earwires
- Bail-making pliers
- Bent chain-nose pliers
- Side cutters

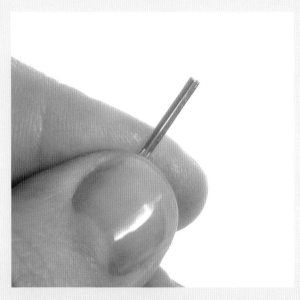

1 Cut 2 pieces of wire about 6" (15.2cm). Cut the ends while holding the wires together, so they're exactly even and flush.

2 Holding the 2 wires together and treating them as 1, create a simple eye loop at the end of the wires using your bail-making pliers.

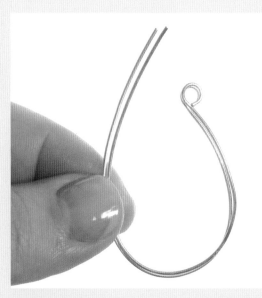

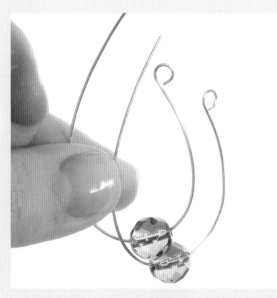

3 Use your fingers to curve the 2 wires, still holding them together, into a gentle U curve. The tails of the wires should extend about ¾" (1.9cm) past the eye loop.

4 Separate the wires, then thread a single bead onto each wire. You may need to open the curve slightly to get the bead directly into the center of the curve. Don't force it or you'll mar the wire—allow gravity to do the work.

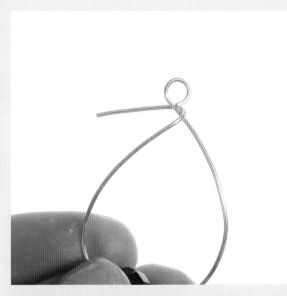

5 Wrap the tail wire around the loop's neck 3 to 5 times, then cut and tuck the wire end down at the back of the earring. Repeat on the second earring, being careful to keep the teardrop shapes intact and identical.

6 Use your bent chain-nose pliers to straighten the neck and tighten the wrap.

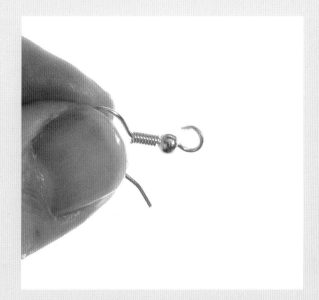

7 Attach earwires to the top loops of both earrings. Open the earwire loop sideways using pliers just like you would to open a jump ring, hook onto the loop at the top of the earring, and close the earwire loop sideways.

Cascading Bead Earrings

Earrings can be made simply and beautifully to coordinate with any outfit, mood or day of the week. Here's where color theory can be the most fun! Dig through your stash of beads and pull out three pairs of beads in a harmonious color scheme (three beads per matched pair); create something flashy or elegant, sizzling or suave.

TOOLS + MATERIALS

- 22ga wire, about 12"–14" (30.5cm–35.6cm)
- Two 4mm beads
- Two 6mm beads
- Two 8mm beads
- 2 earwires
- Bent chain-nose pliers
- Side cutters

design note

For the earrings in the step-by-step photos, I've chosen three sets of sparkly, faceted-round firepolished glass beads in an analogous palette of blues and purples. The two-tone beads are my favorite as they add a vibrant, lively feel to the earrings.

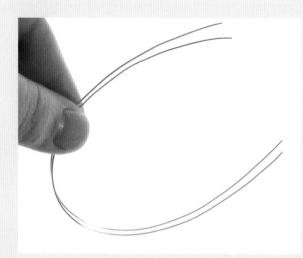

1 Cut 2 pieces of wire about 12" (30.5cm) and cut both ends so they're exactly the same length. Curve them both gently into a U shape with your fingers with a smooth curve at the center.

2 Thread a bead onto the curve of 1 wire.

3 Cross the wire above the bead, leaving a small space above the bead. Pull from the ends of the wires rather than pushing near the bead, to keep the curve smooth. If you push up from the bead, you're more likely to create a bend instead of a curve, which isn't desirable.

4 Twist the wires twice where they cross.

5 Repeat with the second wire. Compare the 2 wires often to ensure they're identical.

6 Thread a second bead onto the left wire of the first earring.

7 Curl the wires up and twist twice where the wires cross. Repeat with the second earring, placing the bead on the right wire. (It's important to get in the habit of creating opposite symmetry at all times when making earrings.)

8 Add a final bead (opposite the second bead) to each earring, and create a single twist at the top. Allow 1 wire to point up and the other off to the side.

9 Create a single curl in the wire pointing up and wrap its tail around the neck tightly, creating a binding wrap.

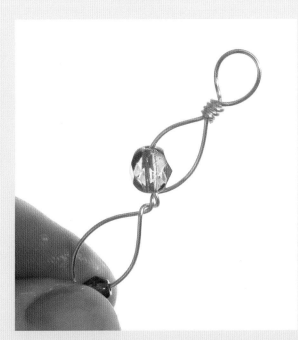

10 Wrap the second wire end around the neck. Keep the wraps tight and close. Cut and tuck both ends to the back of the earring.

11 Complete the other earring, remembering to keep the pieces mirrored, and create the curl in the opposite direction. Attach earwires to the top loop of each earring.

Window Frame Earrings

Begin your exploration into improvisation by working within the constraint of a frame. Build a frame of heavy wire in pretty much any shape, and fill the frame with decorative curls of thinner wire for a gorgeous showpiece. Try the shape shown here first, then experiment with circles, squares and triangles. These earrings also serve as a lesson in mirror symmetry and balance.

TOOLS + MATERIALS

- 18ga wire, about 8"–10" (20.3cm–25.4cm)
- 22ga wire, about 36"–40" (91.4cm–101.6cm)
- 2 earwires
- Bent chain-nose pliers
- Round-nose pliers
- Side cutters

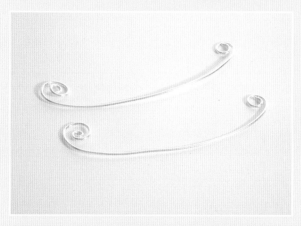

1 Cut 2 pieces of 18ga wire to about 4" (10.2cm). Make sure the pieces are identically sized by cutting the first, and then cutting the second up against it. Create an open spiral at 1 end of each piece of wire.

2 Create a smaller spiral at the other end of each wire. Hold the pieces together to ensure they're the same.

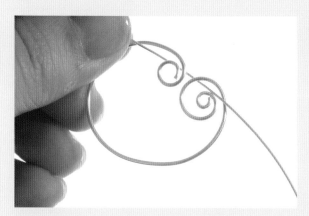

3 Use your fingers to create a soft C bend in the 2 wires. Keep the pieces identical. When the 2 pieces are separated, they should be mirror images in shape, if not exact details. The point is to stay loose and flexible; go with the flow and improvise when you can.

4 Push the curve closed so that the 2 spirals touch. Cut a longer piece of 22ga wire, approximately 18" (45.7cm). Thread about 1" (2.5cm) of wire through the 2 curves where they meet to begin a binding wrap.

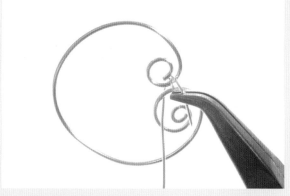

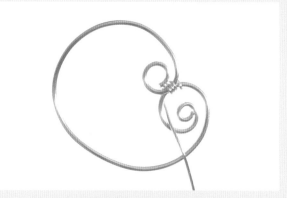

5 Bend the tail end around the 2 wires to begin a wrap that will bind the spirals together. Use your bent chain-nose pliers if necessary to thread the wire through the spirals, and continue the binding wrap.

6 Finish the binding after 3 wraps, and add a final wrap around a single spiral wire. You'll now have a long piece of thin wire attached to an oval frame, which you will use to create decorations.

 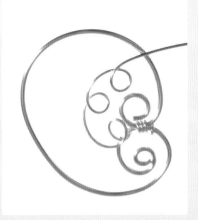 

7 Begin creating curls to fill in the frame in a random pattern. For your first try, feel free to copy the curls shown here, but I encourage you to try your own.

8 Every few curls, create a binding wrap around the frame to secure it.

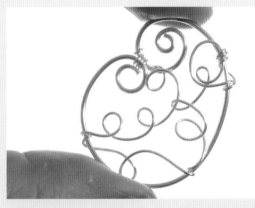 

9 Anywhere the curls meet, thread the wire through to connect them and make it even more secure.

10 Repeat the binding wrap and decorations on the second frame. Note that you don't need to make them the same! Just work towards the same balance of openness vs wire—if you make the curls on the second earring tighter than the first, the 2 frames won't be balanced; try to keep the density the same.

11 Grab a premade fishhook earwire and open the loop sideways with round-nose pliers. Place the frame wire into the open loop. Ensure that the front of the earwire is at the front of the earring frame, then close the earwire loop with round-nose pliers.

12 Repeat with the second earring: remember to make them mirror images of each other.

Curl Burst Earrings

This chic, freeform set of earrings can help you practice your improvisation. There are almost no tools at all in this design! Just wire, your hands, and some pliers to finish it off and add the earwires. Once you've mastered this technique, you'll be able to improvise earrings in nearly any shape. Create something one-of-a-kind to suit your personal style!

TOOLS + MATERIALS

- 22ga wire, about 20"–24" (50.8cm–61cm)
- Bent chain-nose pliers
- Side cutters

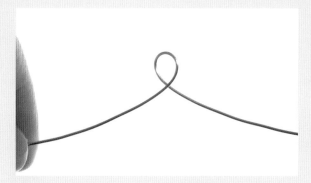

1 Cut 2 pieces of wire exactly the same length, about 10" (25.4cm). Create a loop in the exact center of each wire.

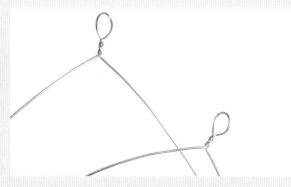

2 Twist the loop where it crosses, creating a "neck" on an eye loop that can be used later for attaching an earwire. This leaves 2 tails on each wire, which can be used to create the decorative curls.

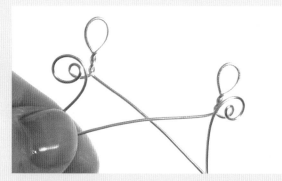

3 Create a double upward curl on the left tail of the left earring wire. Create a double upward curl in the opposite direction on the right tail of the right earring wire.

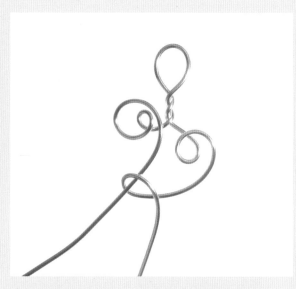

4 On the left earring, create a single downward curl on the right tail. Continue the right tail into a second curl that wraps loosely around the left tail. This will ensure that the 2 tails are integrated tightly for structural purposes.

5 To create symmetrical earrings, it's best to complete each short series of curls on 1 earring and then on the other, alternating so you don't lose your place! So, create a downward curl on the left tail of the right earring, and a second curl around the right tail.

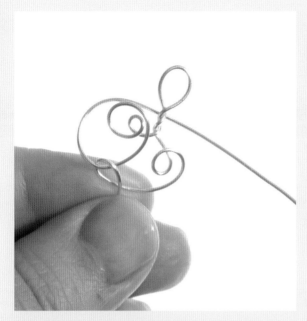

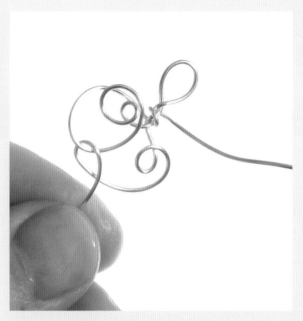

6   On the left earring, continue the left tail's trajectory up and over the double curl, creating a smooth large curl that crosses the neck of the earring. Note: It's usually best to work with the wire's direction, not against it. Repeat in reverse for the right earring (not shown).

7   Wrap the left tail around the neck twice, leaving a short tail of a couple of inches (centimeters). Repeat in reverse for the right earring (not shown).

8   On the left earring, create a single curl opposite its previous curl, then continue it into a double curl that crosses just under that first curl. Repeat in reverse with the right earring. You should now have symmetrically opposite but very similar earrings. Note that they do NOT have to be exactly the same. Again, the density and overall shape are more important than the specific details.

9   On the left earring, create a single outward curl on the longer tail still at the bottom. Repeat in reverse on the right earring (not shown).

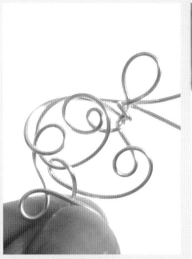

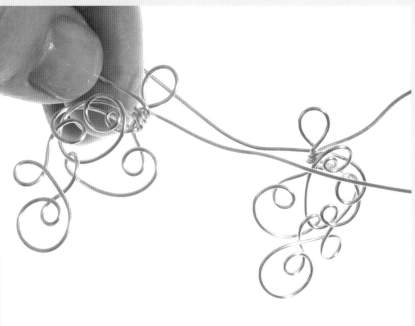

10 Create a single inward curl on the tail, overlapping the previous curls. Then wrap the tail around the neck. Repeat in reverse on the right earring.

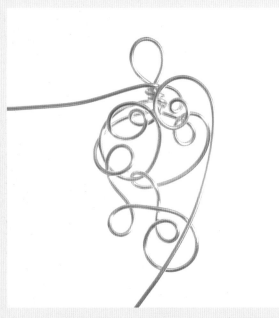

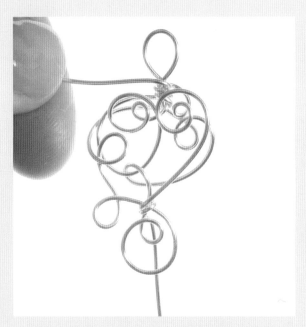

11 On the longest tail on the left earring, create a double inward curl on the right side. Repeat in reverse for the right earring (not shown).

12 Wrap the wire around the place where the large bottom double curl intersects itself, securing this tail. Repeat in reverse for the right earring (not shown).

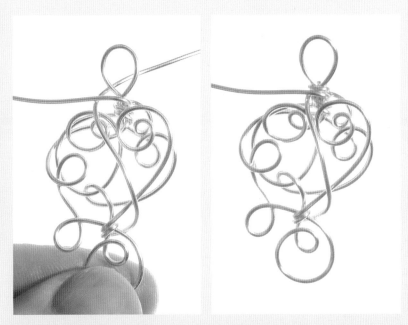

13 Bring the tail up around the front of the earring in an S curve that wraps around the back of the neck yet again. Repeat in reverse for the right earring (not shown).

14 Cut and tuck the smaller tail at the back of the eye loop neck on each earring. Note: The smaller tails on the earrings can also spiraled or integrated further before attaching.

15 Attach the earwires.

Confetti Curl Earrings

This style of earrings is truly fun! Comprised of multiple curls chained together and interwoven with beads, it's an excellent playing field for experiments with color, and for working with organic forms and balance. Your forays into improvising with the practice necklace will serve you well here. As always, follow your instincts and feel free to deviate from the exact design shown.

TOOLS + MATERIALS

- 22ga wire, about 36"–40" (91.4cm–101.6cm)
- 2 earwires
- Two 4mm beads
- Six 6mm beads
- Bent chain-nose pliers
- Side cutters

design note

Choose four pairs of matched beads in an interesting colorway. It's best if there's some variation in the size of the four beads. Here I've chosen a square tetradic colorway of two-tone faceted round firepolished glass beads, in two sizes.

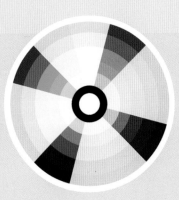

1 Arrange the beads in 2 lines, 1 for each earring. Play with the order of the beads—it's part of the fun! Settle on the most pleasing order.

2 Hold 2 pieces of wire together and cut about 18" (45.7cm), so they're exactly the same length.

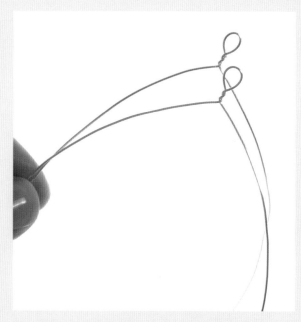

3 Create a curl in the center of each wire.

4 Twist each curl closed 3 times so that you have a twisted eye loop. This will be the top of the earrings where the earwire is attached.

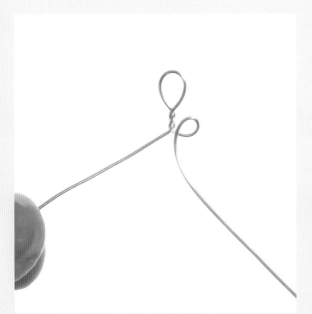

5 Create a small curl pointing out to the right of the neck. This is the left earring. Repeat in reverse for the right earring (not shown). Again, feel free to copy these curls exactly or improvise your own.

6 On the left earring, add a small bead to the left wire and create a small outward curl just after it to trap the bead in place. Repeat in reverse for the right earring (not shown).

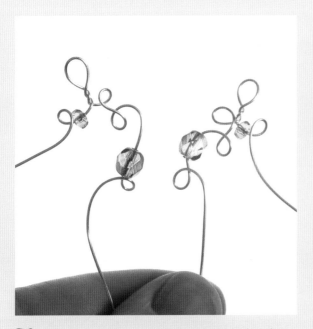

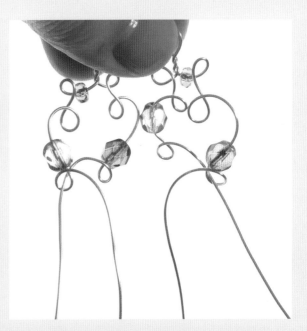

7 For both earrings, on the side without the bead, create a curl pointing in. Thread on a second bead and put in another curl pointing out. Notice the pattern: Alternating curls, alternating beads. The curls both visually frame and structurally support the beads.

8 On the side with the small bead on each earring, create a curl pointing in, thread on a bead, and create a curl pointing out, this time trapping the other tail wire inside the final curl to create an anchor point on both tails.

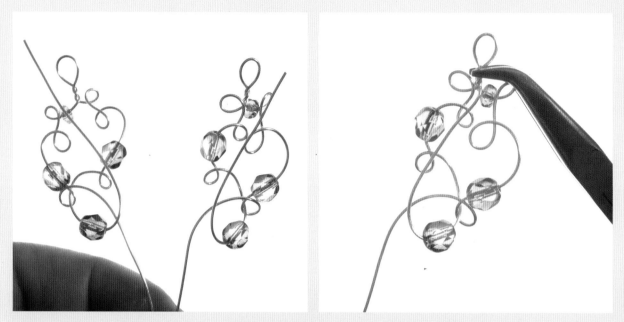

9   On the wire you just trapped, for both earrings, create a gentle curve and thread on the final bead, curving the wire back up towards the neck. Wrap the tail around the neck on each earring. Note: It's important with this organic style that you connect isolated wires together, and that you bring at least 1 of the wire ends back up to wrap around the neck for stability.

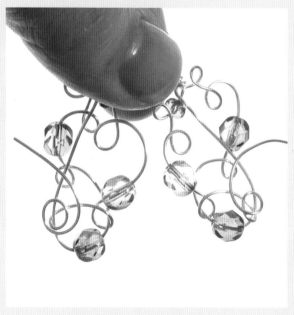

10 Create a double curl on the end wire of each earring.

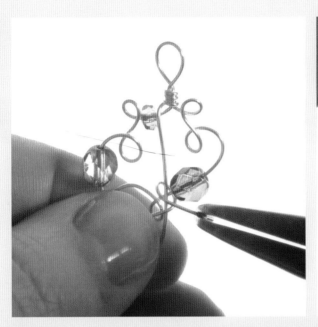

11 The end wires are not long enough to reach back to the neck, so find a place where the wires cross to anchor each tail by creating a binding wrap—in this case, below the second bead added. Ensure that the symmetry is maintained when you complete the second earring.

12 Attach the earwires to the top loop of each earring.

Easy Bead Ring

This humble ring is the ultimate statement of simple style with only one piece of wire and a single bead. The project requires a ring mandrel to shape the ring, but if you can find an alternative mandrel such as a fat marker, dowel, or even a small bottle that creates the right size, that will work as well as the commercial kind. This project will get you used to working on a mandrel.

TOOLS + MATERIALS

- 20ga wire, about 10"–12" (25.4cm–30.5cm)
- One 6mm firepolished bead
- Bent chain-nose pliers
- Side cutters
- Ring mandrel

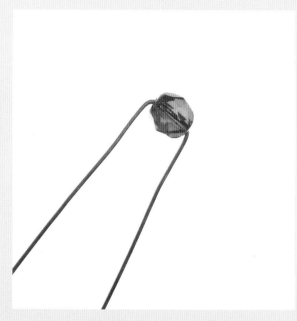

1 Thread the bead onto the center of the wire. Bend the wire down sharply on either side of the bead with your fingers. Make the bends as tight to the bead as possible, but be careful not to exert too much pressure or you may snap the bead.

2 Wrap the wire around the ring mandrel at the your preferred size. The wire will probably slide a little bit as you work with it, but it will even back out.

3 Wrap the wire tails once each around the mandrel until they cross once again over the top, 1 on either side of the bead. You'll have 2 wires across the back as the ring shank, and 3 wires on the top, including the bead wire.

4 Wrap both tail wires around the bead in opposite directions. Keep them as close to the mandrel as possible. Keep your finger on the back of the ring shank at the final size mark so it doesn't slip.

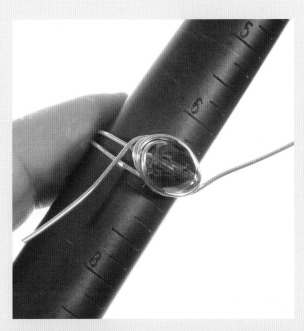

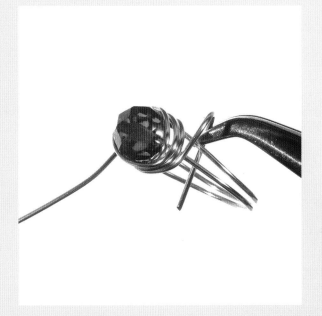

5 Keep wrapping the wires 3–5 times until the edges of the bead are covered. Pull tight with each wrap, but don't allow the wire to slip up over the top of the bead. Keep the wire tails low and tight.

6 Pull the ring off the mandrel. Using your bent chain-nose pliers, curve 1 of the end wires in the same direction as the original wrap through the circle of the ring shank.

7 Pull the wire end through the circle and back up around until it completely wraps the 2 wires of the ring shank. Be careful not to let the shank wires cross over each other. Tighten the wrap with your pliers. Create 2 more wraps until you have 3 total. Cut your wire and tighten it down with your pliers. Repeat the wire wrap on the other side to finish up the ring.

Kaleidoscopic Colors Ring

An extension of the *Easy Bead Ring*, there are a few minor differences and challenges to creating this simple, elegant ring which simulates a classic, channel-set gemstone ring. Use firepolished, faceted glass beads for an inexpensive burst of flash and color. Once you've mastered the technique, try the ring with gemstone beads.

TOOLS + MATERIALS

- 20ga wire, about 10" (25.4cm)
- Two 4mm firepolished faceted glass beads
- One 6mm firepolished faceted glass bead
- Side cutters
- Bent chain-nose pliers
- Ring mandrel

design note

Pull out three beads in your favorite color scheme. Here, I used the Alternative Primary Triad with two-tone beads of purple, yellow, and teal-blue. The beads can be the same size, but I prefer the look of a larger 6mm bead with two 4mm beads on either side.

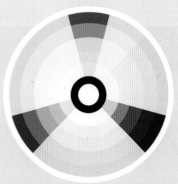

1 String the beads in order onto the wire. Let gravity settle them in the center of the wire.

2 Gently curve the beads up, and bend the wire sharply to either side of them. This is a little trickier than with a single bead; be gentle or you'll kink the wire between the beads.

3 Place the beaded wire onto the ring mandrel at your desired size. Wrap the 2 tail wires around the mandrel, crossing at the back.

4 Bring the tail wires to the front of the mandrel, keeping them parallel (don't cross or twist!). Hold the wires tightly against the steel, until each wire lies against either side of the row of beads.

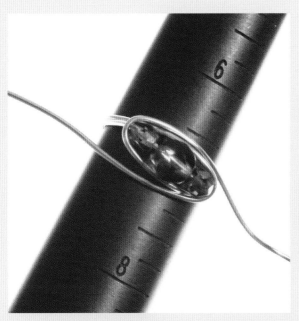

5 Very carefully wrap the wires around the row of beads. Again, this is trickier than with a single bead—the wires have a greater tendency to slip up over the beads. Keep the wires low and close to the mandrel.

6 Wrap the wire several more times around the row of beads, then slide it off the mandrel. The wire tails should be 1"–2" (2.5cm–5.1cm).

7 Use the pliers to wrap the tail ends securely around the ring shank, 3 times each. Cut and tuck the wire down at the top.

Rosette Ring

Another variation on the *Easy Bead Ring*, this project uses organic curls to build a complex-looking setting for an otherwise uncomplicated ring. This is a great starter project; you can practice controlling curls in a project, but it's really only the same curl six times. The result is dazzlingly pretty.

TOOLS + MATERIALS

- 20ga wire about 14"–16" (35.6cm–40.6cm)
- One 6mm firepolished, faceted bead
- Bent chain-nose pliers
- Side cutters
- Ring mandrel

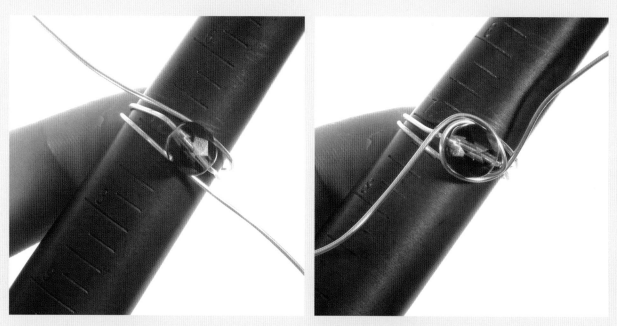

1 Just like with the *Easy Bead Ring*, thread the bead onto wire, bend the wire down on either side, and wrap the wire around the ring mandrel at your preferred size. Wrap the end wires around the bead just once.

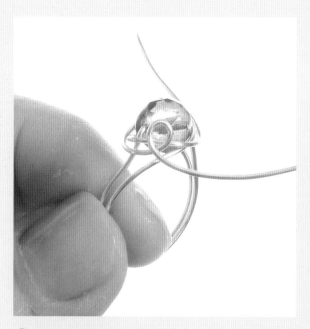

2 With 1 of the wire tails, create a single curl pointing up. The curl should cover about one-third of the side of the bead.

3 Create 2 more curls along the side of the bead in the same direction. The 3 curls should fit fairly evenly along the side of the bead.

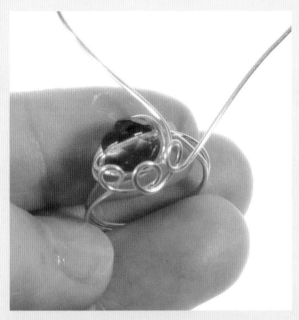

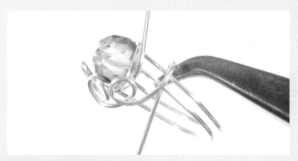

4 Push the curls up against the side of the bead.

5 Just like with the *Easy Bead Ring*, wrap the end of the wire around the ring shank up next to the bead. Wrap the end wire 3 times around the ring shank, cut it off and tamp it down.

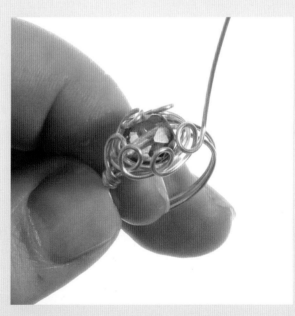

6 Complete the 3 curls on the other side, wrap the end around the shank, and your ring is complete!

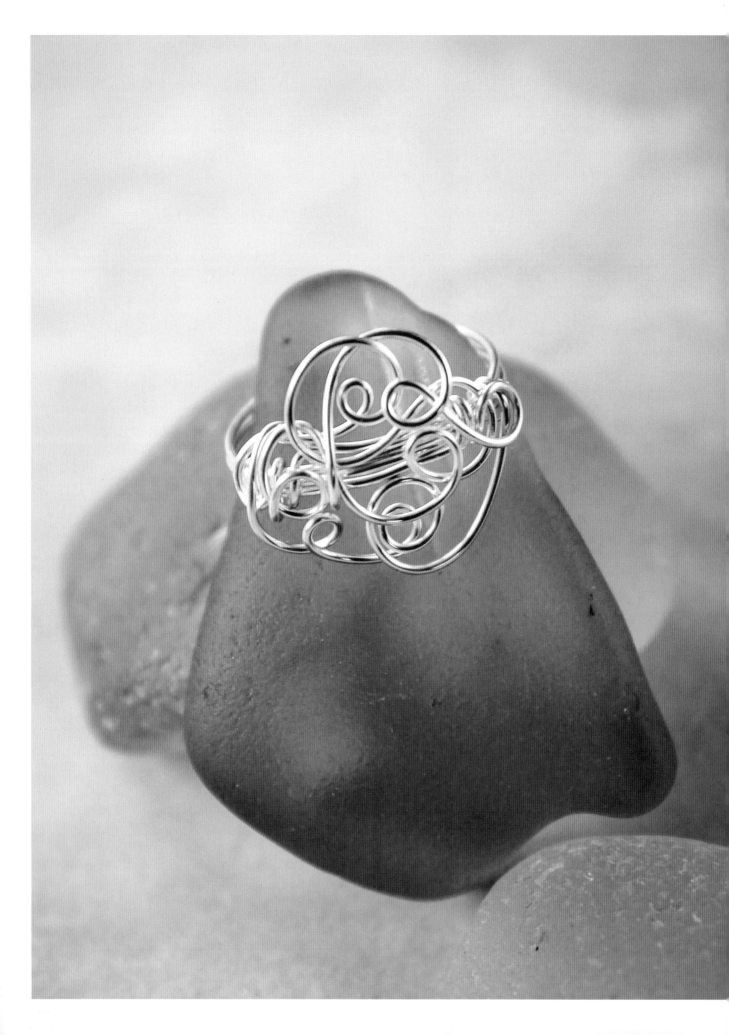

The Million Ring Design: Swirling Wire

Wire rings have nearly endless variations. This technique gives you a solid foundation with room for infinite diversions from the steps to create a ring that's uniquely yours. This ring is the first in two stages leading to a more complex ring. You can either create a wire-only ring or follow through to the end of the next project to have a complete beaded ring that's different from any other.

TOOLS + MATERIALS

- 22ga wire, about 12" (30.5cm)
- Bent chain-nose pliers
- Side cutters
- Ring mandrel

tips & hints

Ring mandrels are round, but fingers are somewhat square. I find ring sizes to be quite variable.

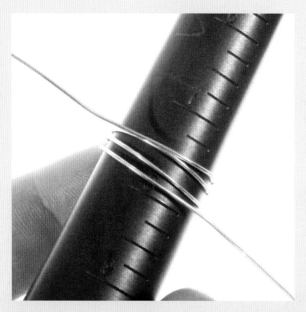

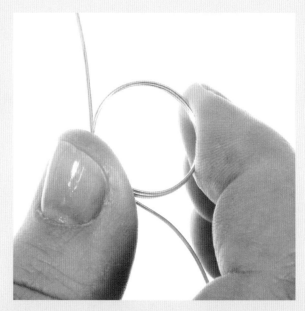

1 Wrap the center of the wire around the mandrel 3 times at or just smaller than your desired ring size. Make sure the wire ends lay next to each other, not crossed; the wire should maintain full contact with the mandrel at all times. The right-hand wire is always above the left-hand wire on the mandrel.

2 Pull on the tails to tighten up the wire and put your thumb on the crossed wires where they meet in the front. Put your index finger on the wires at the back as well. Carefully pull the wire off the mandrel.

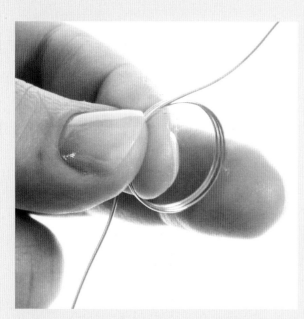

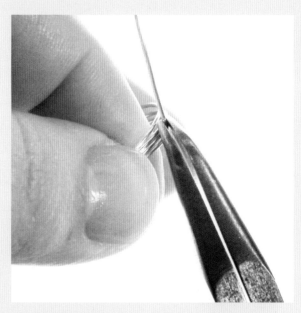

3 The way you hold this unsecured ring shank is important. Hold the place where all the wires cross with your thumb and finger, with your finger inside the ring. Use your middle finger to secure the back of the ring, opposite your thumb.

4 Using your bent chain-nose pliers, bend 1 of the tails at a 90-degree angle over top of the 3 parallel wires.

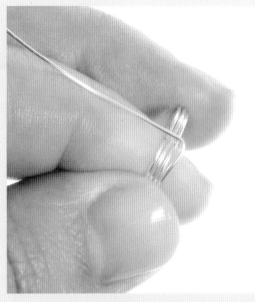

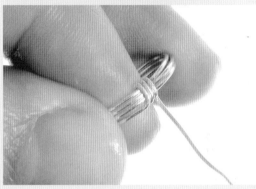

5 Keeping a tight hold on the 3 wires, pull the tail behind and through the center of the ring with your fingers. Tighten the tail around the ring shank and complete 3 binding wraps.

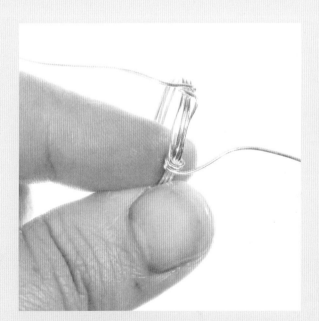

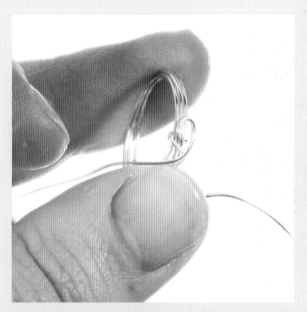

6 Flip the ring around 180 degrees on your finger and repeat steps 4 and 5 with the second tail end of wire. Depending on the size of your ring and how far across the surface of the ring-top you want your design to run, you can put the wraps farther from or closer to the first one. Your design will extend slightly beyond the edges of the wrap, so keep that in mind too!

7 Hold the ring as before and grasp the top-most tail of wire, which should be pointing off to your left. Bend the tail in a simple curl away from the wraps (clockwise). This is the start of your decorative base.

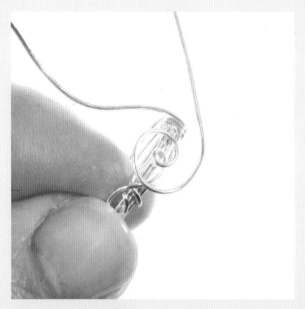

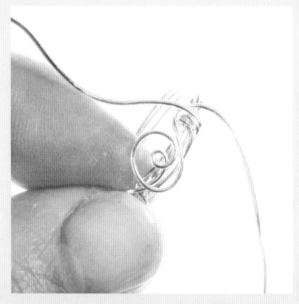

8 Continue to make flat curls along the top of the space between the wraps, in any pattern you like.

9 Holding your decorative curls flat to the top of the ring, tuck the end of your tail wire through the ring, up against the wrap on the opposite side. Curl the wire clockwise around and behind the other tail wire.

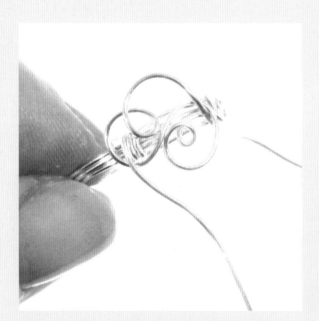

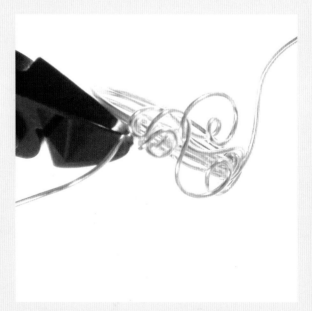

10 Turn the ring to the left and create a single inward curl. Feed the end of the wire through one of the existing curls—interlocking helps secure both wires.

11 Create a couple more curls at the end of the design (back where you started), then create a binding wrap. Cut and tamp down the wire tail at the top.

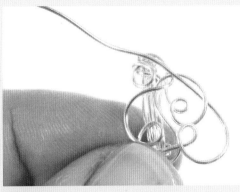

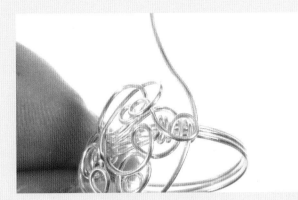

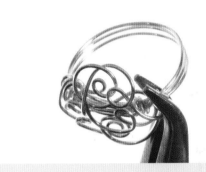

12 With the other wire tail, create a series of curls down the ring. Improvise! Create interlocking tails and curls where possible within the design to secure the top.

13 When you reach the other side again, leave about 1" (2.5cm) of the tail for the final wrap, then cut and tamp it down. This is what I call a ring base, as it's a base for further decoration if you'd like!

note

If your ring is too large, use bent-nose pliers to make a small S-bend in the shank of the ring, under the curls.

14 Slip the ring base back onto the ring mandrel. Depending on how tightly you were able to hold onto it in the beginning, you might find the ring has increased or decreased in size. If it's too small (which is the most likely situation with the addition of the wraps), push it just a little further onto the mandrel to stretch it out. This has the added benefit of work-hardening the wire.

73

The Million Ring Design:
Color Cascade

This ring is the second stage of a two-stage design. Complete the *Swirling Wire Ring* (see the previous project), and use it as a base on which to "sew" some beads for decoration, creating a sparkling, vibrant ring that is both comfortable to wear and captivating to the eye.

TOOLS + MATERIALS

- 24 or 26ga wire, about 14"–16" (35.6cm–40.6cm)
- Four 4mm fire-polished glass faceted beads
- One 6mm fire-polished glass faceted bead
- Bent chain-nose pliers
- Side cutters

design note

The beads I've chosen for this project come from the Alternate Modified Triadic color scheme—pink, orange, and green.

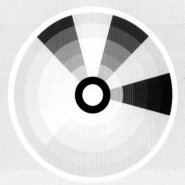

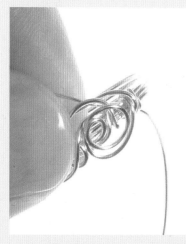

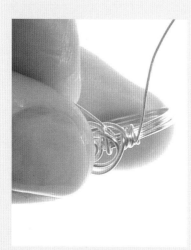

1 Complete the *Swirling Wire* ring in the previous project to use as a base. Thread the end of the wire through 1 of the end loops on the base ring so that it passes through both a loop and the ring itself. Leave a small tail of about 1" (2.5cm) on the side of the ring.

2 Create a binding wrap with the wire tail tightly around the ring shank. Don't cut it yet; it'll stay more secure this way for now.

3 Thread the beads—in this case, a 6mm bead with two 4mm beads on either side—onto the long tail of the wire.

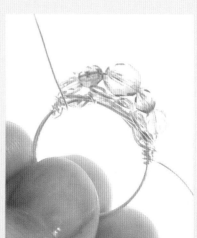

4 Bend the long end of your wire around the ring base to secure it, leaving the beads flat across the wire curls. Don't keep the beads next to the base while you do this, as the wire may kink. Instead, lift up the whole wire, beads and all, and pivot from the lowest bead. Tuck the tail wire into a loop and through the ring base at the other side.

5 Gently pull the wire through until the bead at the opposite end is snug against the face of the ring. Make sure none of the beads have slipped out of place. Bend the wire and row of beads down over the top of the wire curl base, and wrap the long tail around the ring shank, up close to the curls. You may need to curve the wire into an S shape to make it fit, or choose beads that will fit perfectly if you want a straight line.

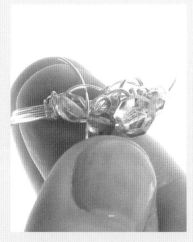

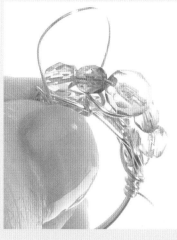

To prevent kinks in the wire, thread in large curls. Keep your finger inside the loop until it's closed if you find it has a tendency to kink. Go slowly and patiently.

6 Bring the long tail over the gap between the 4mm beads, and wrap the long tail up and around the ring shank, between the first bead and the second. Thread the wire between the ring shank and the wire curls, so that the wraps are close, tight and hidden.

7 Pull the wire tight so that it sits in the gap between the 4mm beads and has made a full loop around the ring base.

8 Continue wrapping the wire between the line of beads and around the ring shank, "sewing" the beads down. Pull the wire as tightly as you can.

9 When you reach the end of the line of beads, wrap the wire tail around the ring shank once or twice. Turn the wire in the other direction and wrap back to the starting point, this time in the opposite direction, creating a subtle X pattern at the base of each bead.

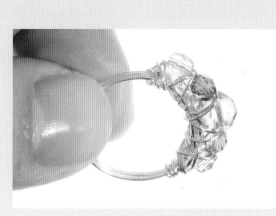

10 Cut the wire tails and tamp them into the sides of the ring shank.

Speedy Bead Pendant

If you're like me, you're interested in wire because you've got a stash of gorgeous focal beads you don't know what to do with. Here's a simple way to create a pendant out of a single, knockout bead such as this artisan-made lampwork bead. Use this technique to showcase nearly any bead.

For this project, I'm using specialty bail-making pliers, but you can use your largest round-nose pliers or even a smooth-barrelled pen.

TOOLS + MATERIALS

- 20ga wire, about 8"–10" (20.3cm–25.4cm)
- Large focal bead
- Bail-making pliers
- Bent chain-nose pliers
- Side cutters

design note

The bead featured in this necklace was made by Amy Houston of Two Glassy Ladies.

1 Wrap the bottom 2" (5.1cm) of the wire twice around your chosen mandrel or the bail-making pliers.

2 Wrap the tail of the wire around the neck to bind it, as close to the mandrel as possible. You can use your hands to get this started.

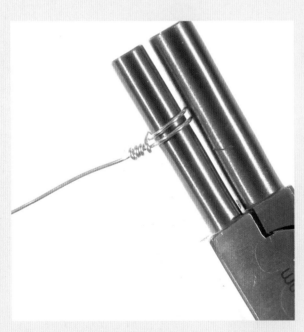

3 Use the bent chain-nose pliers to finish the wrap and tighten it up.

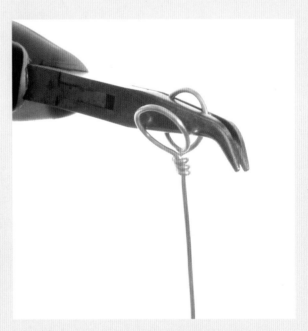

4 Pull the wire loops off the mandrel, and open the loops gently with bent chain-nose pliers to finish off the bail.

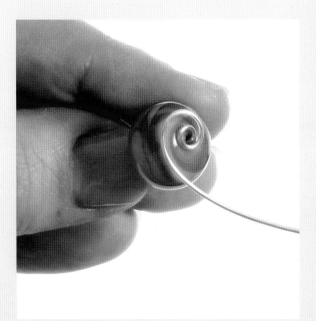

5 Slide your bead onto the end of the wire and push it up to the bail.

6 Create a double curl at the bottom of the bead; push it close up to the bead with your finger.

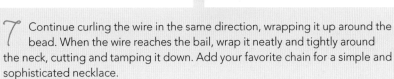

7 Continue curling the wire in the same direction, wrapping it up around the bead. When the wire reaches the bail, wrap it neatly and tightly around the neck, cutting and tamping it down. Add your favorite chain for a simple and sophisticated necklace.

Steps of Light Pendant

I'm a big fan of techniques that are easily reproduced but still allow for infinite variations. This simple pendant is one such technique! The basic process is fairly intuitive and lends itself well to more intricate decorations: simply cut a longer piece of wire and curl as you go.

I call this the *Steps of Light Pendant* because the linear pattern of faceted Czech glass beads is brilliant when it catches the light.

TOOLS + MATERIALS

- 20 or 22ga wire, about 10"–14" (25.4cm–35.6cm)
- Faceted round glass beads: 2mm, 4mm and/or 6mm, in any colorway
- Bail-making pliers
- Bent chain-nose pliers
- Flat-nose pliers
- Side cutters

design note

For this necklace, I've chosen a Traditional Split Complementary color scheme of orange-brown, teal-green, and blue.

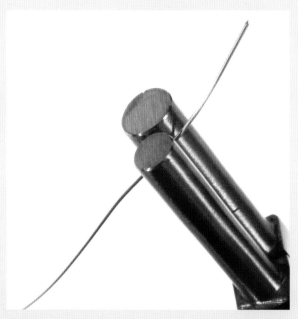

1 Gently grasp 1 end of the wire between the 2 barrels of the bail-making pliers, about 1"–2" (2.5cm–5.1cm) down from the end.

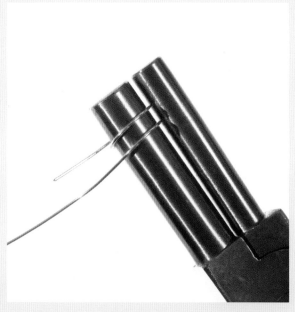

2 Wrap the wire twice around the larger of the pliers' barrels. You'll have to open the pliers slightly for the second loop. The wire may slip a bit; as long as the barrels aren't tapered, you're fine.

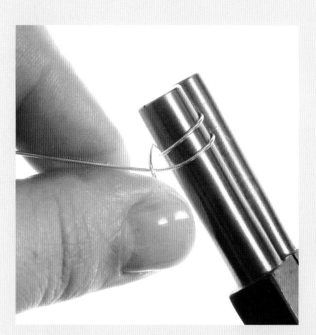

3 Use your fingers to begin a wrap of the short tail around the longer tail, while keeping the wire on the pliers.

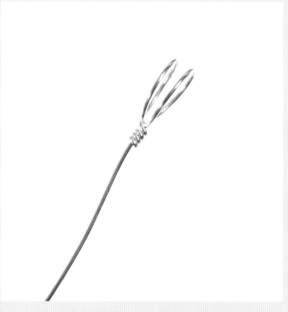

4 Use your bent chain-nose pliers to complete a tight binding wrap. Cut and tamp down the end, and slide the double wrap off the bail-making pliers to reveal your rabbit-ear bail.

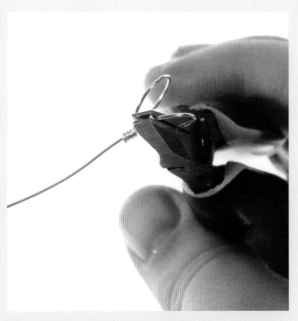

5   Open the loops slightly with your flat-nose pliers.

6   Thread the beads onto the wire tail in your preferred order. This section of the wire will be referred to as the "stem."

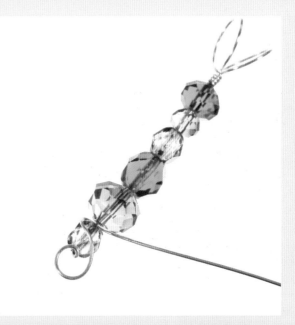

7   Create a tight single curl in the wire at the end of the last bead to secure the end of the stem. Carry the wire up and over a second time into a double curl. Let the tail wire sit crossing the stem wire between the last 2 beads, pushing the second-to-last bead up slightly.

8   Grasp the bottom bead and the curl together, and holding the wire tight to the bead to stabilize the curve in the wire, wrap the wire around the back of the stem, between the bottom 2 beads. The tail wire should be wrapped tight against the stem wire, in between the bottom 2 beads.

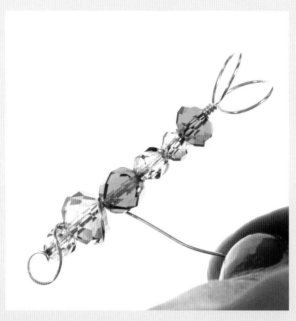

9 Using your fingers, gently curve the tail wire up and over the second-to-last bead towards the next junction between beads.

10 Grasp the wire against the second-to-last bead to hold the curve tight and stable. Again, wrap the tail wire around the stem wire, in between the fifth and fourth beads.

11 Continue this pattern of curving the tail wire up and over each bead and wrapping it around the stem wire in between that bead and the next one, until you reach the top of the pendant (the bail).

12 Wrap the tail wire tightly around the binding wrap you made earlier, at the base of the bail. Continue wrapping the tail wire around the bail neck until you reach the top of the twist and can't wrap any further. Keep your wrapped loops tight close, and even.

13 Pull the tail wire to the front of the pendant, and use your fingers to gently curve it over the first bead and down. Cross the wire over the last wrap you made on the way up to make an X or create your own pattern: this is a very freeform style of wire wrapping and nothing is wrong.

14 Continue wrapping the wire around each bead by crossing over the front of the bead and wrapping around the back of the stem, until you reach the last junction between beads.

15 Wrap the wire around the last junction a couple of times to secure it. Cut the wire close to the pendant. Gently tamp the wire down using bent chain-nose pliers.

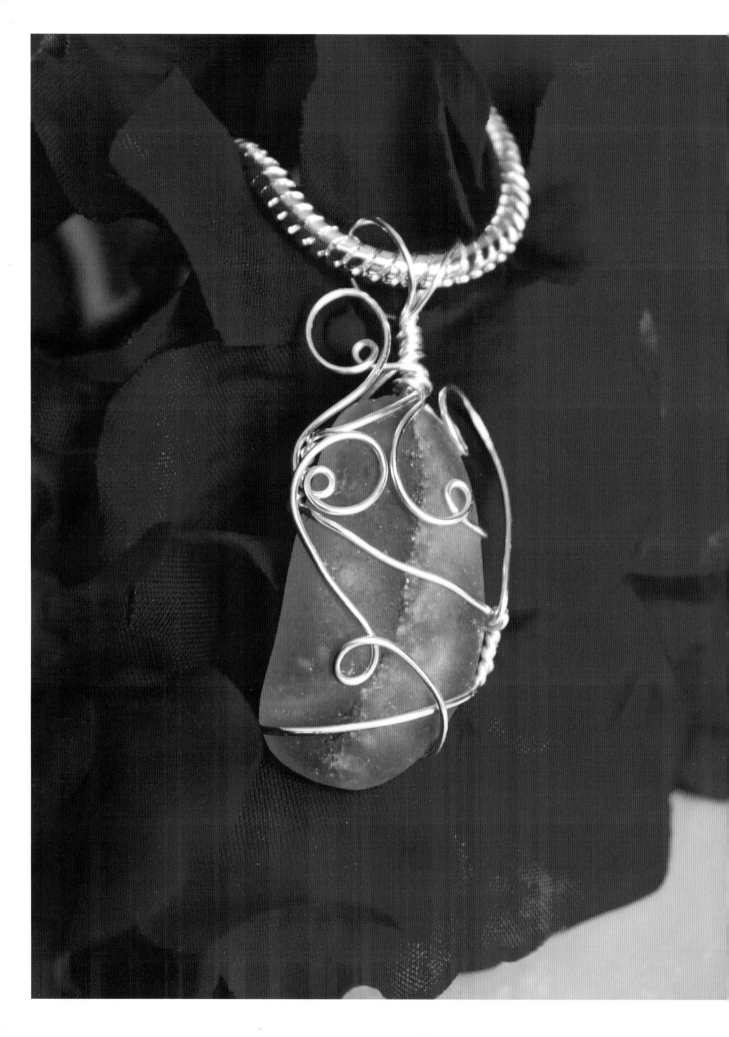

Twist-and-Shout Pendant

Beach glass, or sea glass, is one of the prettiest pieces of trash around. I am lucky to live on Cape Breton Island in the Atlantic Ocean where I'm able to collect my own beach glass. If you aren't so lucky, you can buy beach glass at online auction sites or buy simulated beach glass.

The twist technique gives a solid, structurally safe wrap for any flat, irregular object. Beach glass works well because its surface is naturally rough—shiny, polished objects are pretty but very slippery, and therefore much more difficult to control.

TOOLS + MATERIALS

- 22ga wire, about 24" (61cm)
- Beach glass
- Bail-making pliers
- Bent chain-nose pliers
- Flat-nose pliers
- Side cutters

design note

Take some time to decide what will be the front and back of the stone, and which way you want the stone to hang when you're done. You might want it to hang like a teardrop or a shark's tooth. Putting the larger chunk of stone at the top will help you keep it sturdy in the beginning; however, as you get better, you'll be able to make the stone hang any way you like!

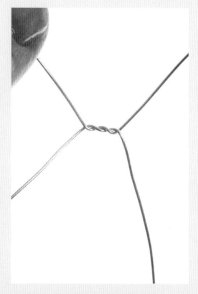

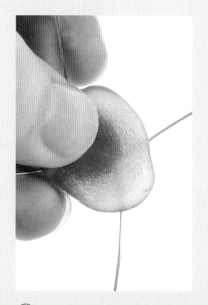

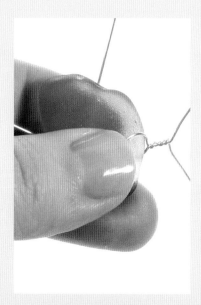

1 Cut 2 wires, about 24" (61cm) and twist the centers together. Using the twist technique from the *Basic Wire Techniques* section, complete 3–5 twists in the center of your crossed wires. This will be the initial twist, or spine.

2 Grasp the stone in the orientation you've chosen (front first, top up). Place the twist at the back of the stone.

3 Wrap one of the "legs" of the twist across the front of the stone to meet its opposite counterpart. Twist the wires together tightly 5 times.

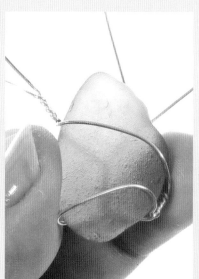

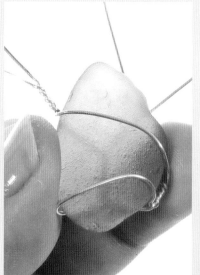

4 Push the twist up against the front or side of the stone, so that the twist runs from the top to the bottom of the stone. Push tight! Keep the wire as close to the stone as possible.

5 Pull the wires across the front and back of the stone, creating another X-shaped intersection. Twist those together as well, up against the side of the stone. Note: You may need to rotate the stone slightly to reach the edges to twist; be sure to keep your fingers and wire tight to the stone to keep it from slipping. Again, push the twist against the front or side of the stone, up towards the top.

6 Continue connecting and twisting the wires on opposite sides of the stone until you reach the top. This stone didn't require many twist maneuvers, but a larger stone would.

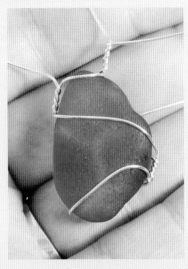

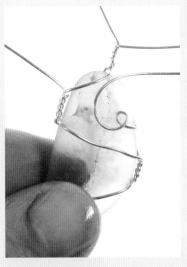

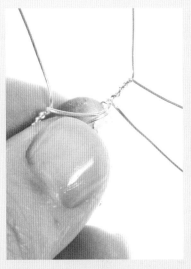

7 Take a wire from the front of the stone and one from the opposite side on the back, and twist them at the top of the beach glass to create the stem for a bail.

8 Near the top of the stone, use one of the back wires to create an integrated double curl across the front of the stone.

9 Hold the double curl flat and tight to the front of the stone, then wrap its tail tight around the wrap at the top of the stone.

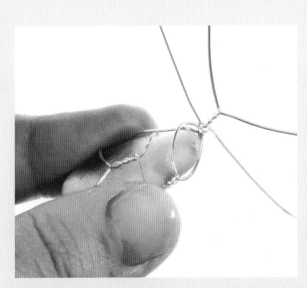

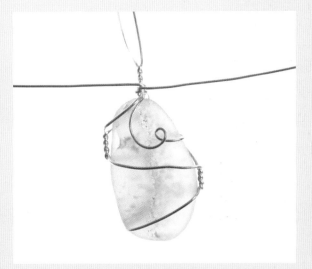

10 Pull some or all of the remaining wires around the stone and wrap them around the bail twist at the top. Note: Make the wrap-around the tightest you can. Pulling the wire is easier than pushing it, and longer wire is easier to work with than shorter.

11 So long as the stone is relatively secure, you can leave a wire for decoration later on, such as I've done here. If your stone feels a little loose, don't worry, you'll be tightening the wires in the next step. If the stone is very unstable, wrap an extra wire around the entire stone, securing it at the top.

12 Wrap the 2 wires at the neck around the outside barrel of the bail-making pliers' jaw; the wires should be going in opposite directions.

13 Point the 2 bail wires opposite each another: 1 facing front and 1 back. Place the correct-size jaw of your bail-making pliers perpendicular to the wires— the same way a chain would go. Put it into the V of the wires as far as you can.

14 Without removing the pliers, wrap the ends of the wires around the stem of the bail. This will be the final layer of wire, so make the wraps neat and close together.

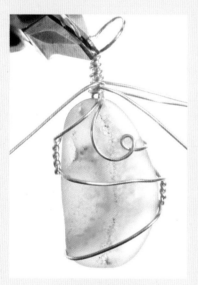 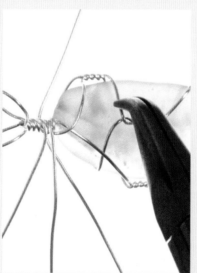 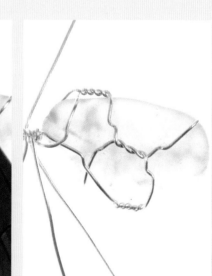

15 Use your fingernails to separate the bail loops to create a pleasing Y shape. The bail loops are probably a little wobbly, so use the widest part of your flattest pliers to give them a gentle squeeze along the loop's surface.

16 At this point, the wire cage around the beach glass is probably pretty loose. Use your bent chain-nose pliers to create an S-curve on each of the back wires. This will tighten the whole cage and keep the stone in place. Be careful to hold the other wires down so you don't twist them out of shape. Be especially careful of the curls on the front.

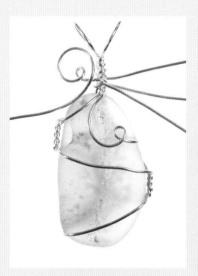

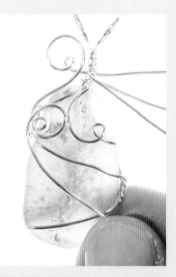

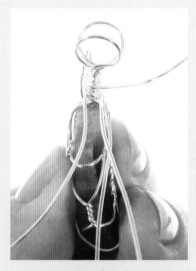

17 Now it's time to add some more decoration. Take 1 of the tail wires near the front of the pendant and make a double curl up near the neck of the bail.

18 Create a second double curl in the opposite direction, along the face of the stone.

19 Pull the wire down to the bottom of the stone, around and up the back; wrap it around the neck. It should feel secure and balanced, like it won't slip.

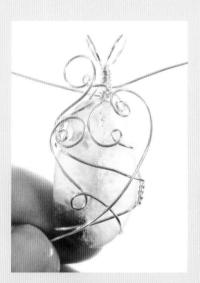

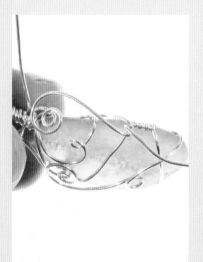

20 On the other side of the stone, with 1 of the remaining tail wires, create a small, swooping, double curl that curves down to the opposite side of the stone.

21 Twist this wire around a wire already secure on the stone: Figure out the basic placement of the wire, then gently pull the loose wire around the secured wire. Hold the double curl in place, and pull the wire through, creating a single wrap around the base wire. Clip the loose wire close to the base and use flat-nose pliers to clamp down the end.

22 With 1 of the remaining tail wires, create a single curl, bend it down the front of the stone, around the bottom, and up the back. Secure it by wrapping it around the neck then cutting and tamping it down at the back of the bail's neck.

23 Since the design looks balanced, the final tail wire will not be used. Cut it close to the bail's neck and tamp it down at the back of the bail's neck.

Double Strand Pendant

A refined technique, working with two wires adds sparkling complexity to your designs. Despite how intricate a double-wire design looks, it couldn't be easier to do. The key is to keep the wires flat and together, treating them as one and using your fingers to keep the wires parallel.

This project will also teach you how to create a new type of bail that can be done without a mandrel, as well as how to focus on the decorative wire instead of the structural wire.

TOOLS + MATERIALS

- 22ga wire, about 24"–36" (61cm–91.4cm)
- A medium-size, flat gemstone bead, drilled top to bottom with a hole sized to fit 22ga wire
- Bent chain-nose pliers
- Side cutters

design note

Choose a nice, flat gemstone bead such as this 1½" (3.8cm) Rutilated Quartz irregular faceted piece. The trick to getting truly stunning results is to use a bead. Because it's pre-drilled, you have less to worry about structurally; the wire through the bead and surrounding it will ensure that the bead stays nice and secure, allowing you to focus on the decoration.

1 Find the middle of the wire by touching the ends together; bend the wire loosely in half at the midpoint. Tighten the bend into a hairpin with your fingers.

2 Use bent-chain nose pliers to really tighten up the hairpin—be careful, the wire can wriggle, so it's best if you keep your fingers close to the pliers.

3 Holding the wire double, create a single curl in the wire, about 1" (2.5cm) from the hairpin.

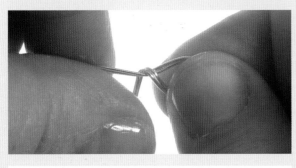

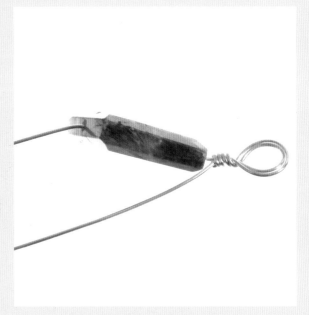

4 Create a binding wrap of the tail end of the hairpin around the longer wire where they cross. This is the beginning of the bail. We'll finish it later.

5 Thread the bead onto 1 of the wires and push it all the way up to the neck of the bail.

6 Bend the second wire along the back of the bead and bend it up to meet with the wire as it protrudes out the hole at the bottom.

7 Grasp the 2 wires flat in your hands and make a single curl. Run your thumb across the top of the 2 wires to keep them flat and parallel throughout the whole curl—it should be 1 smooth, continuous motion. You may find it easier to move both hands at once.

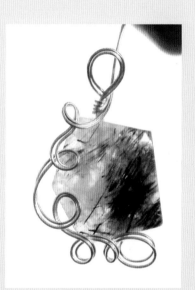

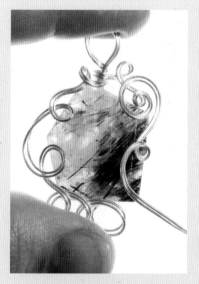

8 Run some free-form decorative curls up the side of the bead. Note how I'm alternating outer and inner curls and hugging the bead to create the illusion that these curls are what's holding the stone in place.

9 An important part of this style is to secure the wire as often as possible without compromising the design. Wrap the 2 wires tightly and flatly once around the neck of the pre-bail you made earlier.

10 Run a complementary set of improvised curls down the other side of the bead. Check the balance of the design after every curl or 2 to ensure you're showing off the bead to its best.

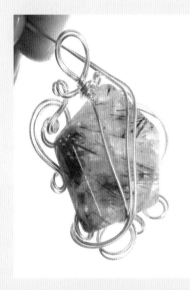

11 When you get to the bottom, tuck the long wire end around the wires gathered at the bottom of the bead, then bring the doubled wires up the back of the bead. This will add continued structure to the piece. Wrap the tail wires around the neck.

12 With your fingers, turn the pre-made bail 90 degrees so its face is now perpendicular to the rest of the loops. Spread the 2 wire loops apart like rabbit ears. Use your fingernail to separate them if necessary.

13 The loop that was on the outer/top edge of the doubled loop will be longer than the other, by the height of 1 width of wire. To reduce the height, twist this single loop around 180 degrees.

14 With the flat edge of your pliers, gently flatten the rabbit ear loops front to back to remove any curves or wobbles. Don't press too hard! A gentle squish is enough.

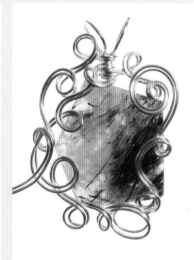

15 If you still have tail wire remaining, use it to create another layer of freeform curls running down the side of the stone. This layer will be more open and swirling to contrast with the tight curls of the first layer. Anchor the final layer by occasionally threading the wire through the base layer. As always, feel free to improvise with your own designs on these curls.

16 Create a large double curl at the bottom to balance out the bail at the top.

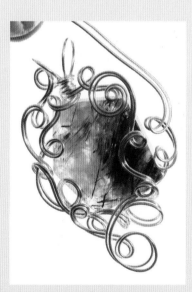

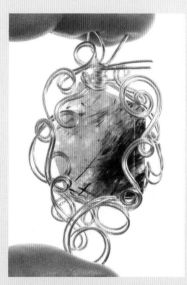

17 Continue the second layer of curls up the other side of the bead, balancing the overall look and creating a pleasing layer.

18 Wrap the end of the wire around the neck at the top. This will be front and center on the pendant so ensure that the wrap is tight, close, parallel and neat.

19 Cut and tuck the wire ends into the back of the bail's neck, tightly and carefully, using bent chain-nose pliers. The pendant is complete!

Braided Jewel

As a wire wrapper, I'm constantly looking for ways to make the wrap better, easier, and more beautiful. Using a braid to wrap stones is not always the most stable—three wires are off-balance and unsteady. It suddenly occurred to me to try to adapt a four-strand braid for wire! After some experimentation, I've pretty well perfected it—and you can, too!

Like most of my techniques, this one gives you a solid foundation and allows for infinite diversions from the main steps to create a design that's uniquely yours.

TOOLS + MATERIALS

- 20 or 22ga wire, about 36" (91.4cm)
- 1 stone (somewhat flat and thick, like a low-dome cabochon)
- Bent chain-nose pliers
- Flat-nose pliers
- Side cutters
- Stationary hook

1 Cut 2 pieces of wire about 14"–18" (35.6cm–45.7cm) depending on the size of your stone. Stack the 2 wires next to each other and create a flat curl in the center.

2 Grasp the curl between your thumb and finger and create a twist about ¾" (1.9cm) down from the curl. Twist 3 times to create the neck of the pendant. This is a variation on the rabbit-ear bail from the previous pendant; it also gives you something to hold onto while you create the braid.

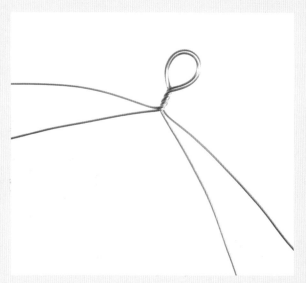 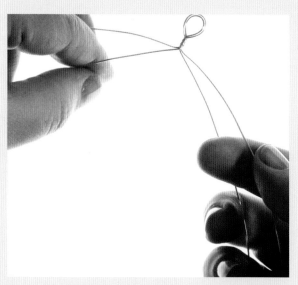

3 Separate the 4 tail wires so there are 2 wires on each side. Slide the loop onto a stationary hook such as a pegboard hook, cup hook, or thumbtack (not pictured).

4 Insert the index finger of your left hand into the space between the 2 left wires, from the front. Your middle finger and thumb will sandwich the 2 wires between themselves and your index finger.

Insert the index finger of your right hand into the space between the 2 right wires, from the back. Again, your middle finger and thumb will sandwich the other 2 wires.

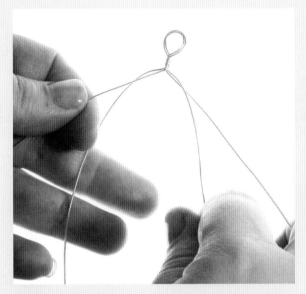

5 Twist your wrists counterclockwise so that your left palm now faces up and your right palm now faces down. More importantly, you've crossed the right-hand wires in each of the pairs over the left-hand wires.

6 Before moving your hands, cross the left-middle wire over the right-middle wire. With practice, you can do this all in 1 motion, using your ring fingers to execute the cross as your other fingers complete the twist. This motion is called twist-and-cross.

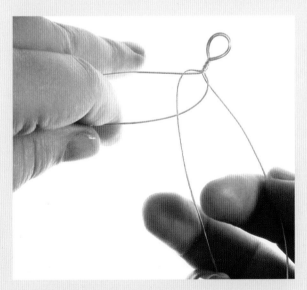

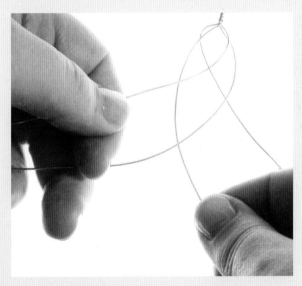

7 Take your fingers out from between the wires and gently pull the wires up so the twists and crosses get pushed up a bit. You've completed the twist-and-cross technique! To continue, return your hands to the starting position: insert your left index finger into the front of the pair of wires on the left, and your right index finger into the back of the pair of wires on the right.

8 Repeat the twist-and-cross (steps 5 and 6). You can see the braid starting to form! Again, gently pull on the wires to push the braid up a bit.

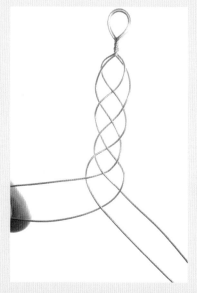

9   Continue the twist-and-cross technique until the length of braid is about twice the height of the stone you want to wrap.

10   Pull the loop off the hook and adjust the braid to make it more even. Measure the length of the braid by rolling the stone's edge (or circumference) loosely along it. If necessary, add or remove links in the braid until it fits perfectly around the edge of the stone. Place the loop neck at the top of the stone, with the flat of the braid against the side of the stone.

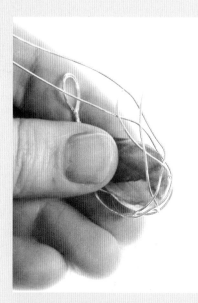

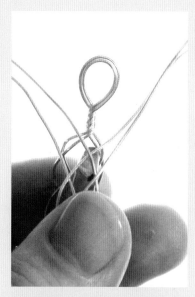

11   Tuck the flat part of the braid into the curves of the stone's edge, and bend it flat around the corners and curves. When the braid fits tightly all the way around, the tails should meet the neck of the loop.

12   Separate the 4 tails, 2 on either side, so that the inner 2 meet up against the neck of the loop.

13 Wrap the wire tails tightly around the neck. Be sure to keep the braid tight around the stone. Keep your thumb on the braid side to keep it from pulling out of shape. Leave the 2 sets of double wires for now.

14 Use your fingers to push the outer edges of the braid out, over, and down against the front and back of the stone, all the way around, to capture the front and back of the stone. Press gently and keep the braid loops even.

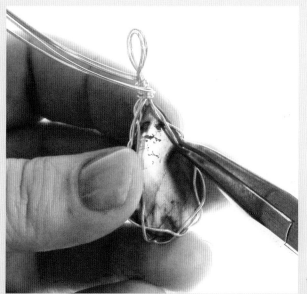

15 Use chain-nose or bent chain-nose pliers to gently create sharp bends in each of the loops on the back of the stone. Bend the loops in the same direction if you can. Don't overdo the depth of the bends, or you will pull the wire off the front of the stone. When you get to the bottom, be careful to keep the spacing even; it can more easily be pulled out of shape here.

16 Using your fingers or wide, flat pliers, gently pull out soft curves on the front of the stone. Be careful not to pull the wires off the back of the stone. At the neck, you'll want to really pull out those wires; you may need to apply some force but be careful not to break or scratch the stone.

17 Create the bail. See steps 12–14 of the *Double Strand Pendant*.

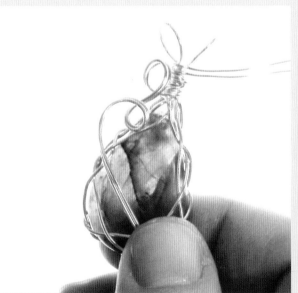

18 Treat each wire pair as a single wire in order to decorate the front and sides of the stone. Your stone may require a different set of decorations; feel free to improvise! Make an outer loop, then an inner loop. Curve the tails along the front of the stone and tuck them up underneath one of the braid wires.

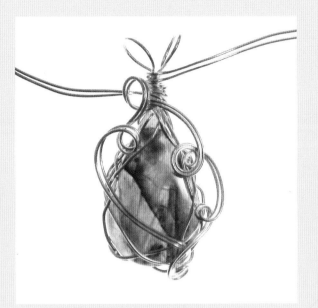

19 Create a double loop where the wire passes through the braid wire—be careful to keep the wire flat to the stone, don't let the braid warp—then create an inner loop and a double inner loop up the other side of the stone. Where the wire meets the neck, wrap it tightly to secure the design.

20 With the other doubled wire, create a second layer of loops. In this example, a single inner loop leads the wire behind the stone, emerging bottom center to create a large double loop.

21 Continue with an inner loop in a graceful curve, an outer loop that tucks in over the existing loops, and curve the wire around to the back. Bring the wire up the back to the neck. Wrap the wire tightly and neatly around the neck. Trim both double wires and tamp them down.

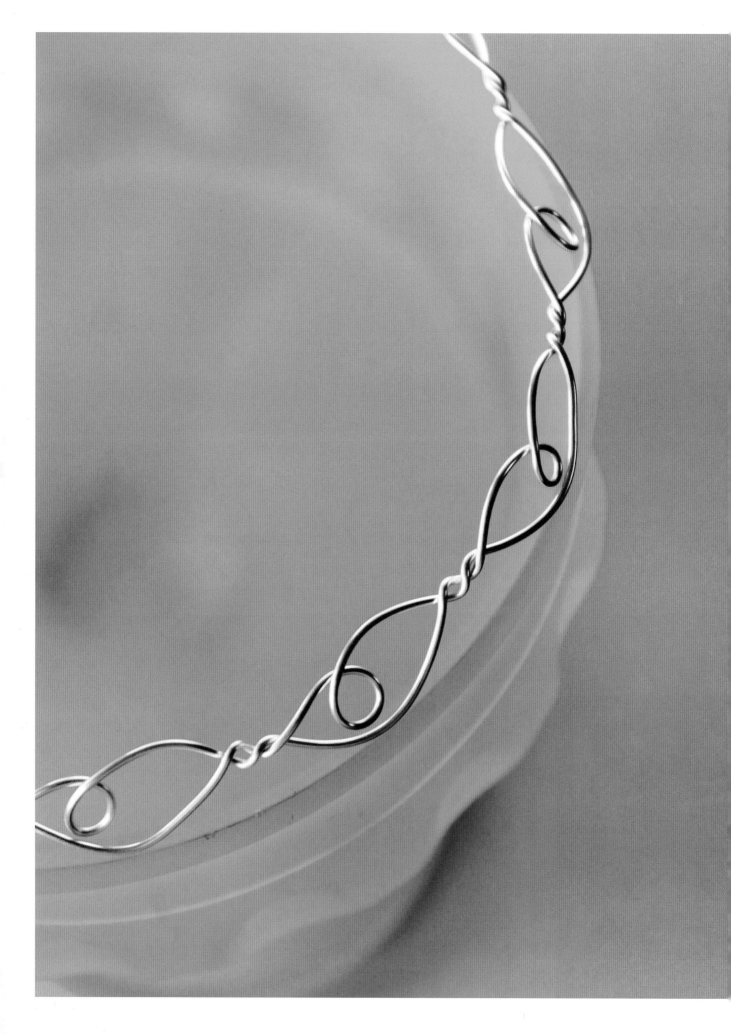

Handwoven Neck Wire:
Silver Eye

Sometimes a chain just isn't fancy or substantial enough. And when you use nontarnish artistic wire, especially in unusual colors, it can be frustrating when your findings don't match your work. So, after plenty of experimentation I came up with an easily repeatable and measurable method of creating a lovely, sturdy alternative to premade chains! The final product can be the base for a more elaborate neckpiece (created by wiring further decorations on top, as seen in the *Statement Necklace*), or you can use a commercial bail to create an interchangeable alternative to a chain.

design notes

When working without tools, it's important to hold and control the wire very loosely. If you hold too tightly you'll kink the wire and it will be difficult to fix. It should be simple to lightly control the wire without bending it unduly.

Working with wire this long can get a little wild. Don't let loved ones get poked in the eye!

Use a commercial bail that is easily opened and closed to attach a pendant to your neck wire, if desired.

TOOLS + MATERIALS

- 18ga wire (4 times the desired length of your finished design, at least 64" [162.6cm])
- Bail-making pliers (optional)
- Flat- or bent chain-nose pliers
- Side cutters
- Hammering surface or anvil
- Nylon or rubber hammer/mallet
- Round-nose pliers

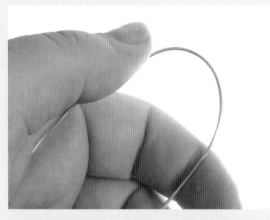

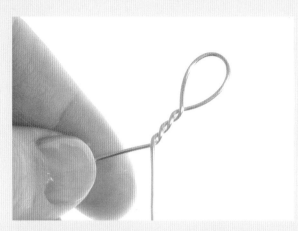

1 Find the center of your wire by folding it in half. Use your fingers to create a loose loop.

2 Close the loop a little more tightly to about ½" to ¼" (1.3cm to 6mm). Create a twist in the wire at the X where the 2 ends cross. Twist 3 times, closing off what is now an eye loop.

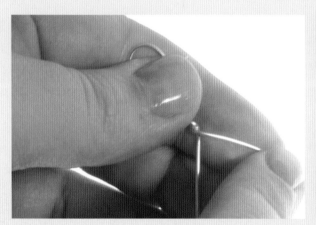

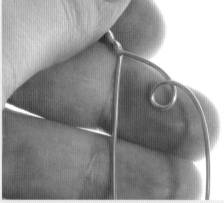

3 At about ½" (1.3cm) from the twist, create a curl in the top wire. Use your index fingers in the center of the loop, on either side of the wire, to keep the loop in control. Use your dominant hand (I'm right-handed) to gently pull the wire around—your dominant hand will rotate about 180 degrees.

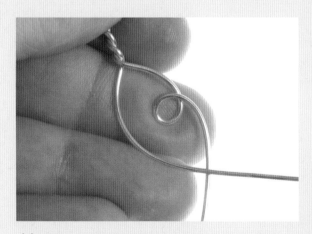

4 Pull up the bottom wire to create an "eye" shape. Adjust the 2 wires until the curl is about in the center of the eye.

5 Create a twist where the wires cross. Twist twice only. Be sure you're happy with the eye shape before you twist; the twist will lock it down.

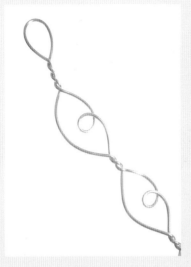
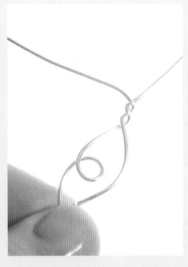
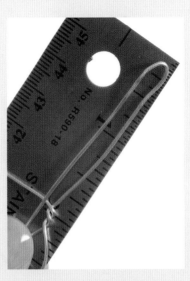

6 Repeat steps 3–5 until you have as many eyes as there are inches in your final length, minus 1. In this case, since I'm building a 16" (40.6cm) neck wire, I'm stopping at 15 eyes. The clasp will make up the final length.

7 Time to make the clasp! This process builds an unbreakable, integrated clasp. At the end of the necklace, bend 1 of the wires out to the side and straighten out the other.

8 Create a U bend about 2" (5.1cm) from the last twist on the straight wire.

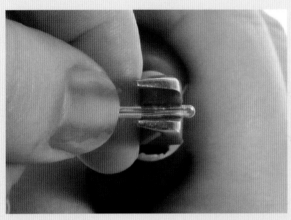
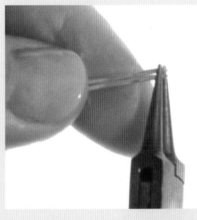

9 Use your bent chain-nose pliers to carefully push the ends of the U-bend together. The wire might be slippery; just be careful and go slowly.

10 Grasp the very tip of the U bend with the very tip of your smallest round-nose pliers.

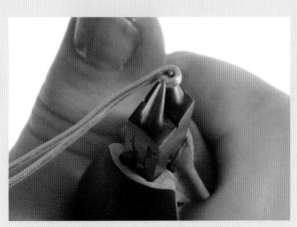

11 With a sharp flick of your pliers/wrist, create a tiny P at the end of the U bend.

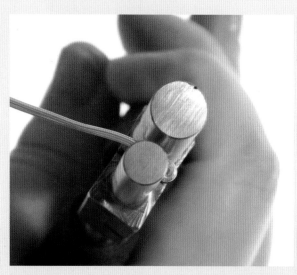

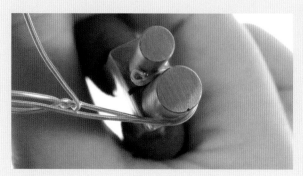

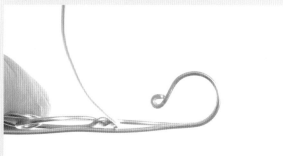

12 Take your fattest round-nose or bail-making pliers and grasp the U bend just below the P shape.

13 Again, with a twist of the wrist, create a large loop in the wire to create the clasp hook.

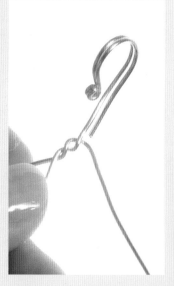

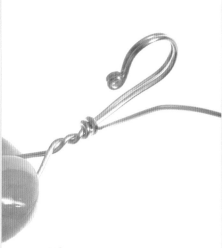

14 Cut the straight wire left over from the U bend, just at or above the twist.

15 Take the remaining wire end and wrap it tightly around the 2 wires in the U bend, being sure to catch the cut end within the wrap. Wrap slowly and be careful not to allow the U-bend wires to twist or cross over each other.

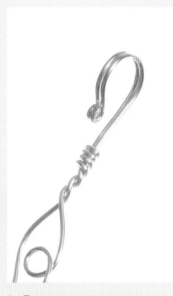

16 Cut the wire close and tuck it in on the inside of the clasp.

17 The neck wire should now be the right length (give or take a ¼" [6mm]). Using a nylon or rubber hammer or mallet (so as not to mar the wire), hammer the entire neck wire flat along its length. It will curve slightly as you hammer; it will also strengthen the wire. Do this twice, once on either side: start with the clasp up first so that the second side ends with the clasp on the outside of the curve.

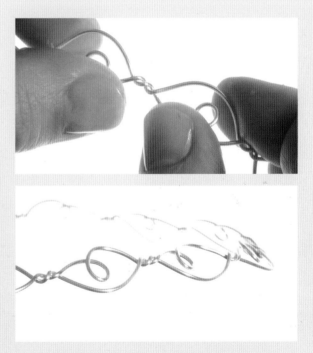

18 Hook the clasp into the eye loop at the other end and create a smooth circle with the neck wire using your hands.

19 Finally, curve out the bottom half of the neck wire so that the whole thing splays slightly outward at the bottom. This will make it sit more comfortably on the neck.

Handwoven Neck Wire: Sparkling Eye

The *Silver Eye Handwoven Neck Wire* from the previous project can be customized to suit any pendant by adding matching beads; or decorate it to work on its own without any pendant at all. This fetching little design sits just at the collarbone and is both cheerful and colorful. Experiment with 7"–8" (17.8cm–20.3cm) lengths of wire for a matching bracelet.

TOOLS + MATERIALS

- *Handwoven Neck Wire* from the previous project
- Various sizes of beads, approximately 1–2 per finished 1" (2.5cm) of neck wire
- 24ga wire 2½ times the length of the finished neck wire
- Bent chain-nose pliers
- Side cutters

design note

For this necklace, I chose a Rectangle Triadic scheme from the alternative wheel.

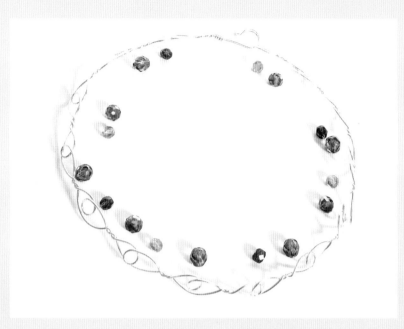

1 Loosely place the beads in a pattern around the edge of the neck wire. About 1–2 beads per 1" (2.5cm) is good.

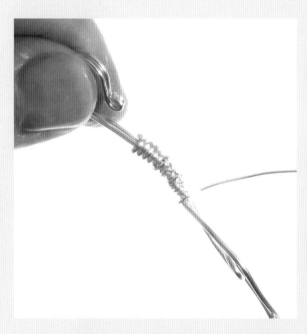

2 Attach the new wire to the neck wire by wrapping the last 1"–2" (2.5cm–5.1cm) of the wire around the coil next to the clasp.

3 Slide the first bead onto the end of the wire and place it into a space within the "eye" on the neckwire. Wrap the wire loosely a couple of times around one side of the eye wires. Work the wire down into and around the twist.

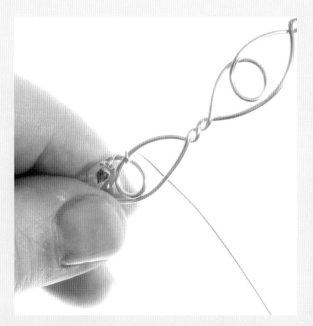

4 Add the next bead to the wire and attach it to the
piece, either at the twist or within the eye. I like
doing it randomly. Just note that wherever the last wrap
ended, that's where the bead is likely to sit.

5 Continue adding beads to the wire along the
length of the neck wire. Secure the wire as often as
possible, both before and after each bead at least, to
keep the beads firmly where you want them.

6 When you reach the other end of the neckwire,
finish off by wrapping the new wire tightly around
the neck of the clasp. Cut the wire and tamp down
the end. You may need to reshape the wire a bit to fit
properly around your neck.

Tumbling Twists Bib Necklace

You can combine a series of stones, such as these small, soft, beach glass pieces, using the twist wrap method to create a charming little bib choker with chain ends that will fit under a shirt collar or sit comfortably over a turtleneck. Choose an uneven number of small, flat stones. Beach glass, with its grippy surface, is definitely the best choice of stone for this method, but feel free to play with other materials!

TOOLS + MATERIALS

- 22ga wire, about 48"–60" (121.9cm–152.4cm)
- 5–7 small pieces of beach glass or other small, flat stones
- A pre-made curb chain necklace
- 2 small jump rings
- Bent chain-nose pliers
- Side cutters

design note

These pieces of beach glass are each about the size of a thumbnail. I've used an analogous color scheme reminiscent of the sea.

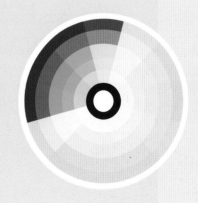

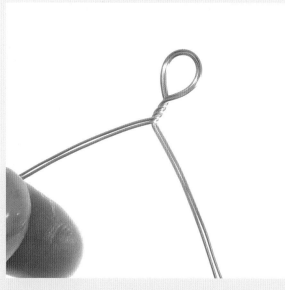

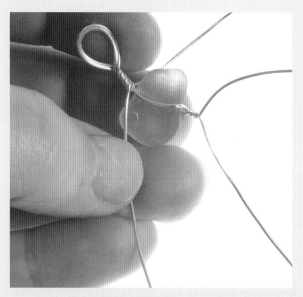

1 Cut 2 pieces of wire about 24" (61cm) long. Treating the 2 wires as 1, create a single loop in the center of the wires, and twist it shut.

2 Separate the 4 wires. Using a wire from the front and 1 from the back, wrap the wires around the front and back of the first stone and twist it closely on the other side. Part of this technique involves feeling out the balance of the irregular stones, so don't be discouraged if the first try doesn't work!

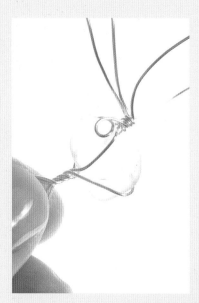

3 Pull the other pair of wires around the stone in a different direction; do your best to ensure that at least 3 sides of the stone are structurally encased in wire. Create a decorative loop on the front wire and then twist the 2 wires shut on the other side.

4 Insert the next stone between a pair of wires, wrap around, and twist shut.

5 Encase the stone with the other pair of wires and twist shut.

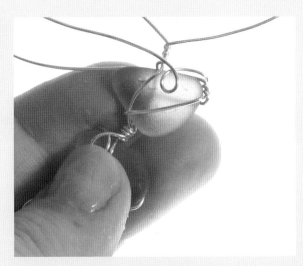

6   Add a decorative loop to the front after the piece is secure, then wrap the tail around the neck of the twist.

7   Make S curves in the wire on the back of the stones with your bent chain-nose pliers to further secure the wraps.

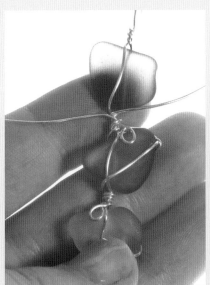

8   Continue adding stones in this method, finding the most secure hold for each using the 2 pairs of wire, and including decorative curls here and there.

9   When the wrap is finished, create a loop that mimics the first in size using 2 of the wires. Tie it off with a wrap around its own neck. Wrap the remaining wires around the neck, as well. Cut the wires and tamp them down.

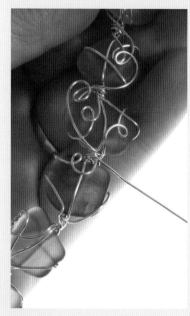

10 Cut about 12" (30.5cm) of wire for the finishing decorations. Wrap the end of the wire around the neck of the loop. The neck of the loop's twist can get messy; add a double twist to disguise it.

11 Continue the wire down the front of the necklace, creating curls where they seem to fit, and securing the wire by wrapping once or twice at each place where the wires twist. Take this opportunity to secure any loose stones with an extra buttress of wire.

12 Finish the wire off at the other loop. Cut and tamp it down. Now you've got the front of a simple necklace! For a quick and easy finish, use a pre-made curb chain to turn this into a wearable piece.

13 Find the center of your curb chain (let gravity do that for you—hold it up by the clasp!), then lay it down gently with the center of the chain at the center of the necklace. Cut where the chain meets the loop's end. Hint: If you want a longer or shorter length than the original chain, cut off more or less!

14 Using the largest jump ring that will fit into a link on your curb chain, attach each loop of the wrap to 1 of the chain pieces.

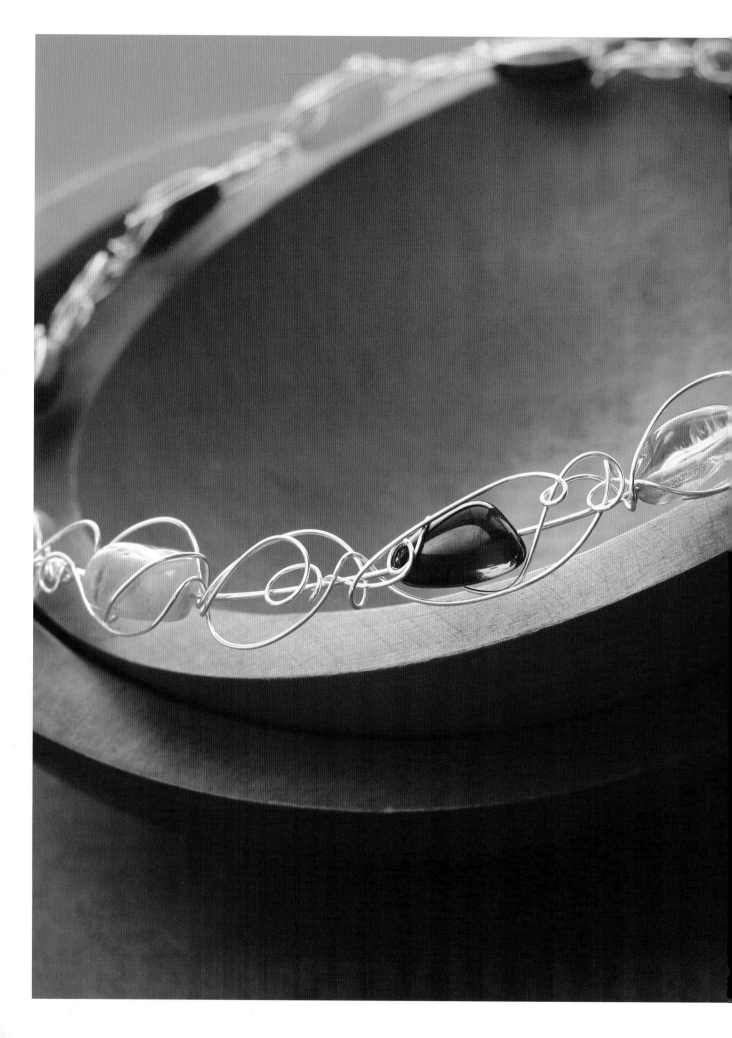

Captured Strand Necklace

A strand of multicolored nugget gemstone beads almost always looks best when kept together, rather than separating each bead into its own pendant. This project creates an open, freeform necklace that allows each individual bead to shine while keeping the strand together.

TOOLS + MATERIALS

- 18ga wire, about 24"–30" (61cm–76.2cm) (the length of the final necklace plus 4"–6" [10.2–15.2cm])
- Strand of 10–20 oblong beads, about 1" (2.5cm)
- 22ga wire (4 times the length of the necklace)
- Bail-making pliers (optional)
- Bent chain-nose pliers
- Flat-nose pliers
- Side cutters
- Round-nose pliers

design note

As with the amber shown here, any gemstone that comes in multiple colors is a fascinating blend of the same material in different shades, and they automatically complement each other. Experiment with watermelon tourmaline, ametrine and fluorite as well. Be sure that all the beads you're using have holes to fit 18ga wire!

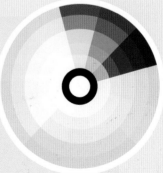

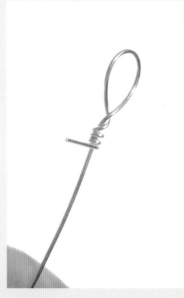

1 About 2" (5.1cm) from the end of the 18ga wire, create a simple wrapped loop either by hand or with tools (by hand is usually faster).

2 Thread the beads onto the 18ga wire, spacing the beads about ¾"–1" (1.9cm–2.5cm) apart.

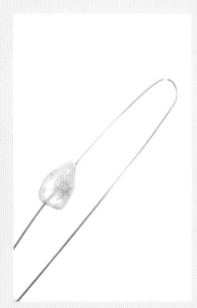

3 Decide the length you want the necklace to be and add 2" (5.1cm). Create a bend in the wire at that point, measuring from the loop at 1 end along the length of the wire.

4 Turn the bend into a hairpin with bent chain-nose pliers. The wire will roll, so hold it close and tight next to the pliers.

5 Using the very tip of your round-nose pliers, make a tiny P from the end of the hairpin. Use flat-nose pliers to even out and tighten the P if necessary.

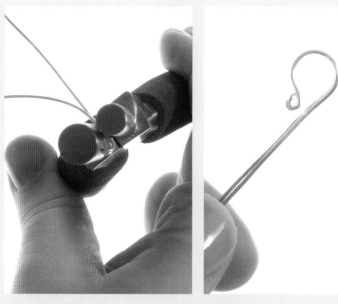 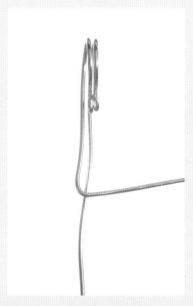

6 Place the P inside your medium-large round-nose pliers or bail-making pliers and wrap the doubled wire away from the P to create a simple clasp.

7 About ¾" (1.9cm) from the bottom of the P, make a 90-degree bend in the left wire, crossing over the right wire.

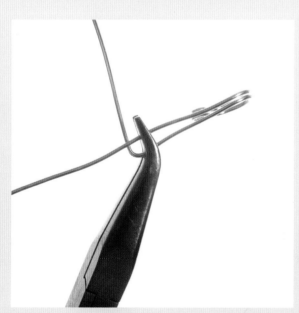 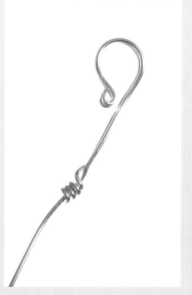

8 Hold the 2 wires flat just above the bend using flat-nose or bent chain-nose pliers.

9 Wrap the tail wire around the other wire tightly 3–5 times. The hook and eye closure is now complete and your necklace is ready to decorate and stabilize.

10　Adjust the beads so that they are spaced evenly along the length of the wire.

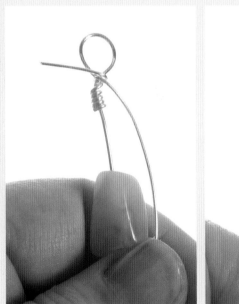  

11　Cut a piece of 22ga wire at least 4 times the length of the necklace. Use a wrap to attach it to the loop end of the necklace; cut the short end and tuck it in.

12　Create a simple curl in the 22ga wire that arcs gracefully over the first bead.

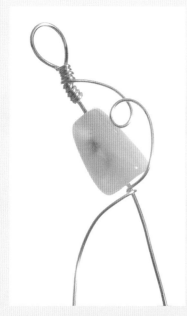

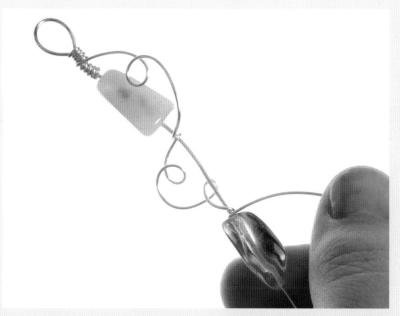

13 On the other side of the bead, create a quick single wrap around the main stem wire.

14 Depending on how many beads you have and how far apart they are spaced, you may need to fill in spaces like I do. If your beads are close together, you can simply decorate over each bead. In this case, create a couple of curls to fill in the space between beads and then a single wrap before the next bead.

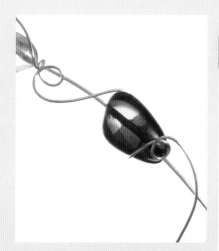

15 Continue creating curls over beads and between beads, with single wraps before and after each bead. The wraps can be tight as before, or loose as shown here.

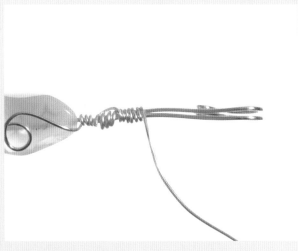

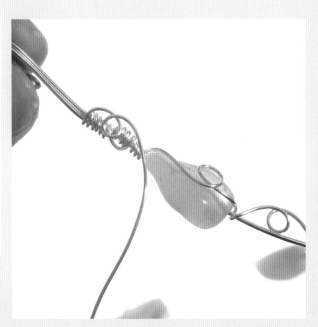

16 When you reach the hook end, take the opportunity to tidy up the wrap and secure this end. Hide any untidiness with some curls in front of the wrap.

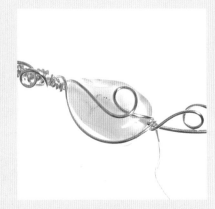

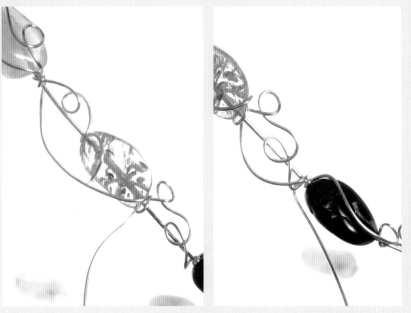

17 You should have a few feet (meters) of wire left, which you'll use to go back down the necklace, creating another layer of decorations. This time, swing a loop below each bead, tying it off before and after each bead with a single wrap.

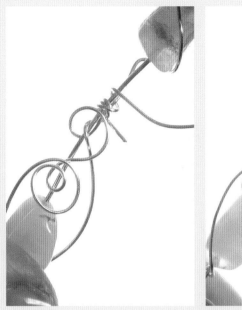 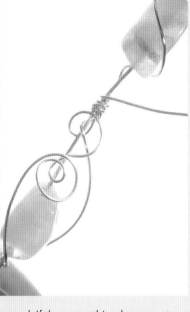 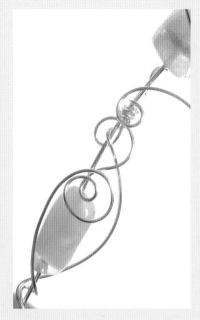

18 I ran out of wire before reaching the end. If the same thing happens to you, here's what to do: First, cut another length of 22ga wire and attach it closely with as neat a wrap as you can make.

19 After the wrap is cut and tucked in, create a curl in front of the wrap to disguise it.

20 Continue down the length of the necklace until there's a graceful curve under each bead/empty space.

21 If you still have wire left, and feel the necklace isn't quite balanced, work back down the necklace once more, this time adding curls anywhere you feel it's unbalanced. When you reach the end of the necklace once more, wrap the wire neatly and secure it. Trim the end of the wire.

Statement Necklace

This necklace is a stunning combination of many techniques you've learned so far plus a few new techniques: color theory, gestalt, basic and decorative techniques are all used in this advanced piece. The result is a captivating, one-of-a-kind necklace that can be customized for any large focal stone.

design note

Examine the colors of your focal stone to identify its color scheme. In this case, my dichroic glass focal stone has an analogous color scheme. Dig through your stash of beads, comparing the colors of beads to the colors of the stone. Collect an assortment of beads in complementary colors.

TOOLS + MATERIALS

- A large, flat, symmetrical focal stone
- An assortment of beads in a complementary colorway, including metal charms
- 18ga wire (2½ times as long as the finished necklace, which should be sized to sit on the collarbone)
- 22ga wire about 10'–15' (3m–4.6m)
- Bent chain-nose pliers
- Side cutters
- Hammering surface or anvil
- Nylon or rubber hammer/mallet
- Round-nose pliers

1 Using the focal stone as a starting point, begin building a mock-up of your layout on a piece of paper or bead board. Create a large grouping of beads (remember the rule of proximity) at the top of the focal stone, then create symmetrically-spaced (but not necessarily symmetrically-composed—remember the rules of similarity and asymmetry) puddles of beads on either side until you have a grouping that is slightly larger than a choker.

Ensure that the color mix is balanced and that you have approximately the same volume of beads in each grouping. Drop in metal charms here and there as accents. For this example, I've used a floral theme with some silver flowers and leaves.

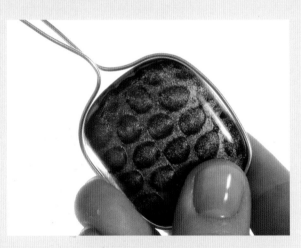

2 Place the center of the 18ga wire at the bottom center of the focal stone, and shape it around the outer edges of the focal stone. When the wire meets at the top of the stone, bend the 2 wires upward in the center. Set this wire aside.

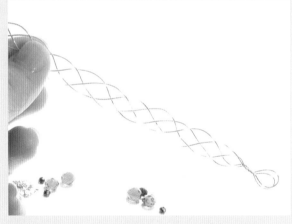

3 Using 22ga wire, create a four-strand braid (see steps 1–9 of *Braided Jewel*) a couple of inches (centimeters) longer than the outer diameter of your focal stone.

4 Once the braid is complete, cut off the loop you used to secure it in the beginning; you don't need it.

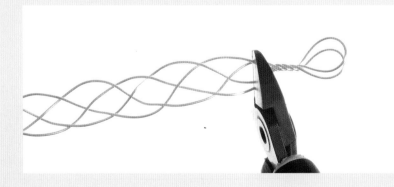

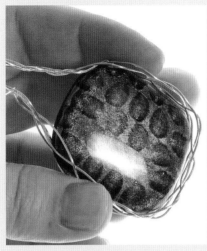

5 Place the center of the braid at the center bottom of the focal stone and wrap it up around the sides of the stone, forming it closely to the shape. (See the *Braided Jewel* for details.) Pinch the braid closed at the top of the focal stone.

6 Cut a piece of 22ga wire a few inches (centimeters) long. Use the center of it as a binding wrap around the braid at the center top of the focal stone. Push it as close to the stone as possible.

7 Shape the braid around the front of the stone, and tighten up the back with pliers. The focal stone should now be secure in its braided setting.

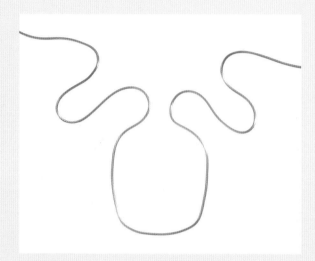

8 Spread out the wires at the top of the binding to keep it from sliding upward.

9 Using the 18ga wire you set aside earlier, create a few symmetrical bends around either side of the focal shape. These can be done by hand or around mandrels or pliers.

10 Create smaller, alternating curves down the length of the wire on both sides to create the base for your design. Leave the last 2"–3" (5.1cm–7.6cm) of each wire alone for now.

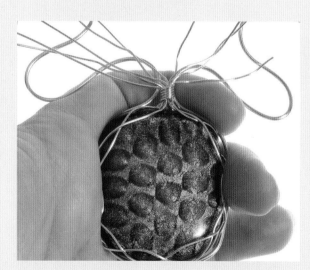

11 Place the heavy wire frame behind the braided focal stone.

12 Hold the frame steady and use 2 of the loose braid wires at the top to bind the focal stone to the frame. Wrap a third wire around to hide any gaps if necessary.

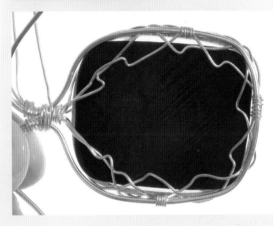

13 Cut small pieces of 22ga wire, about 3"–4" (7.6cm–10.2cm) each, and use them to create binding wraps between the frame and the braid, at the bottom and both sides of the focal stone to secure the frame and braid together.

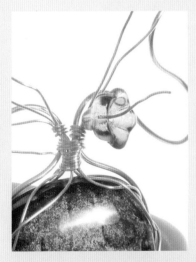

14 On one of the shorter wires (cut 1 wire shorter than the others if you managed to leave them all equal), string on a single bead such as this glass flower.

15 Use your round-nose pliers to create a spiral at the end of the wire that fits tightly up against the bead, securing it in place.

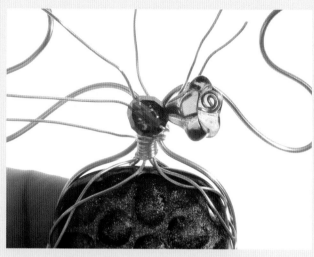

16 Continue adding beads from the focus puddle you built in step 1. Attach the beads with spirals, or if the wire is long enough, add a bead and wrap the end of the wire around the frame. Use as many of the wires as you like. Wrap the wires securely both before and after each bead addition. Keep the wraps neat and hidden behind the beads. Continue adding beads until you're pleased with the arrangement.

17 Finish the ends of all the loose wires, and wrap them tightly against the frame. Smooth down any cut ends at the back.

18 Very lightly hammer the frame's curves; this will work-harden the wire and keep the frame's shape more stable. If your wire has a polycoat, be gentle; hammering could crack and split the coat.

19 Cut a piece of 22ga wire about twice the length of the frame, and wrap the center of it twice around the focal area of the necklace, hiding the join between the beads you added earlier.

Begin making decorative loops around the frame, creating bridges between the empty spaces. Wrap tightly around the frame 2–3 times both before and after each decoration.

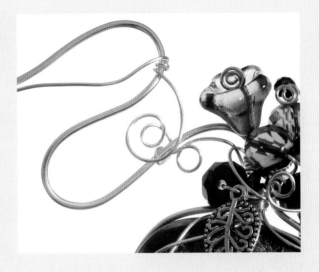

20 Within the decorative curls, start adding beads, again wrapping before and after.

21 Continue wrapping and adding beads. When you are within 2"–3" (5.1cm–7.6cm) of the end of the frame wire, stop the decoration and wrap the wire tightly.

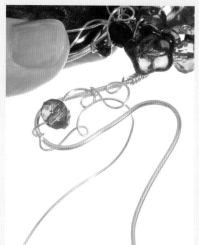

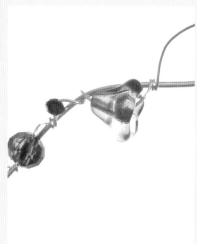

22 Use the other side of the 22ga wire to decorate the other side of the frame, again stopping 2"–3" (5.1cm–7.6cm) short of the end. Compare the 2 sides to ensure they're somewhat symmetrical and balanced, then wrap the wire around the frame to secure it.

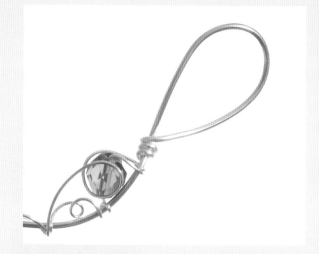

23 Now that the entire frame is decorated, determine your preferred length, then find where the wires cross at that point.

24 Create a U bend in the wire that terminates at the points you just determined, on both ends. You should have teardrop shapes on both ends.

On one side, wrap the end of the wire tightly around the point of the teardrop to create a loop for a clasp.

25 In the other teardrop, cut the wire close to the point of the teardrop, and create a tiny loop or spiral outward to create the hook for a clasp. Open the clasp and lightly hammer the round parts of the teardrops, as well as the tiny spiral at the end of the clasp. You may need to gently flair out the sides of the necklace with your hands to make it fit properly.

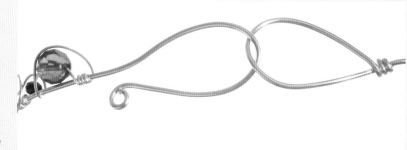

Index

ABOUT THE AUTHOR

Growing up in Cape Breton, Nova Scotia, Gayle's biggest inspiration has always been color: a remarkable sunset, the bonanza of fall foliage, or the subtle shades of the Atlantic Ocean.

As a young girl, she was infatuated with searching for just the right art form, darting from painting to clay sculpting, paper art to web design, digital art to calligraphy and back.

Now, she is delighted to portray her love of color through wire-sculpted art jewelry. More than a decade of self-teaching has gone into developing her distinctive, spontaneous style.

Her pieces weave nontarnish wire around a wide range of stimulating materials. The warmth of semiprecious gemstones, the unlimited colors of variegated firepolished glass and the fascinating textures and history of beach glass all lend their own personality to each one-of-a-kind creation. In her steampunk-inspired line, the patina of vintage, salvaged materials contrast sharply with the bright and modern designs in the surrounding wire.

Gayle's online video and downloadable tutorials have impressed over three-quarters of a million users with her clear, concise, accurate instructions. This is her first full-length publication.

ACKNOWLEDGMENTS

I must thank my talented, helpful, and very professional editing team. Stephanie White and Amelia Johansen, thank you for finding me, encouraging me, and refining me! You never once balked at my seemingly endless questions, and made the process of my first full-length book as simple and painless as possible. Much gratitude to the designer, Julie Barnett, for the gorgeous layout.

Jayme Burns did the beauty shots for this book, and was a delight to work with—we had such fun staging the photos and deciding on the final shots. You made me look good, and I can't thank you enough!

My dear academic colleagues and friends: Scott Sharplin gave me help when I was clearly hopeless at naming the projects; Sheila Christie edited my first online tutorial years ago, helping me refine my teaching style, which led me here. Thank you both for the commiseration and professional advice.

Finally, my delightful husband Laird Hiscock. He never stops making me laugh, never stops encouraging me, and never stops loving me. He always has my thanks for giving me the time and space to pursue what I love. Oh, and for hiring a housekeeper when we're both too busy to mop the floors!

fw
a content + ecommerce company

www.fwmedia.com

19 18 17 16 15   5 4 3 2 1

DISTRIBUTED IN CANADA BY FRASER DIRECT
100 Armstrong Avenue
Georgetown, ON, Canada L7G 5S4
Tel: (905) 877-4411

DISTRIBUTED IN THE U.K. AND EUROPE BY F&W MEDIA INTERNATIONAL
Brunel House, Newton Abbot, Devon, TQ12 4PU, England
Tel: (+44) 1626 323200, Fax: (+44) 1626 323319
Email: enquiries@fwmedia.com

DISTRIBUTED IN AUSTRALIA BY CAPRICORN LINK
P.O. Box 704, S. Windsor NSW, 2756 Australia
Tel: (02) 4560 1600, Fax: (02) 4577 5288
E-mail: books@capricornlink.com.au

SRN: T1865
ISBN-13: 978-1-4402-4133-8

Edited by *Stephanie White*

Designed by *Julie Barnett*

Production coordinated by *Jennifer Bass*

Photography by *Jayme Burns*

METRIC CONVERSION CHART

to convert	to	multiply by
inches	centimeters	2.54
centimeters	inches	0.4
feet	centimeters	30.5
centimeters	feet	0.03
yards	meters	0.9
meters	yards	1.1

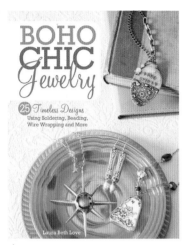
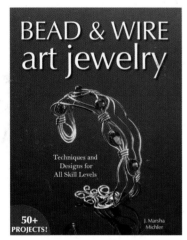